THE LOVE SONGS AND
HEROINES OF
ROBERT BURNS

By the same author

BURNS IN IRVINE (*Lincoln Williams*)
SUN-DIAL SAYINGS (*H. R. Allenson*)
HISTORY OF INNELLAN, ARGYLL (*Kirkwood*)
LINWOOD, PAISLEY AND DISTRICT (*Author*)

ROBERT BURNS

The Love Songs and Heroines of
ROBERT BURNS

REV. JOHN C. HILL, M.A.

WITH 15 PLATES

LONDON
J. M. DENT & SONS LTD

Read the exquisite songs of Burns. In shape each of them has the perfection of the berry; in light the radiance of the dewdrop.

LORD TENNYSON.

Contents

vii

Illustrations

Preface

MANY WHO sing the love songs of Robert Burns have no idea of the heroines in whose honour they were composed. This little book will supply the information. It will also prove useful to those who have to propose a toast to 'Bonie Jean', 'Highland Mary', 'The Lasses', or 'The Immortal Memory of Burns'.

Burns was undoubtedly the greatest song writer this country has ever produced and Love was his favourite theme. 'I never had the least thought or inclination of turning poet', he says, 'till I got once heartily in love, and then rhyme and song were, in a manner, the spontaneous language of my heart.' And writing to his friend Cunningham, he says: 'It is the Alpha and Omega of human enjoyment. All the pleasures, all the happiness of my humble compeers, flow immediately and directly from this delicious source. It is the spark of celestial fire which lights up the wintry hut of poverty, and makes the cheerless mansion warm, comfortable, and gay.'

George Thomson, Burns's publisher, clearly saw the genius of the poet in his songs. In a letter to Burns he says: 'These songs of yours will descend with the music to the latest posterity, and will be fondly cherished so long as genius, taste, and sensibility exist in our island.'

Others may seek titles, or power, or wealth like Lon'on Bank:

> But gie me a cannie hour at e'en,
> My arms about my Dearie, O;
> An' warl'ly cares, an' warl'ly men,
> May a' gae tapsalteerie, O!

There speaks the true Robert Burns.

I am indebted to innumerable sources for information, particularly to Cunningham, Scott Douglas, Blackie & Son, Chambers, and the *Burns Chronicle*.

It should be noted that Burns was not *in love* with all the heroines mentioned in this book. Many of his songs are simply poetic licence. On meeting with any beautiful young lady he pictured himself *in imagination* as being in love with her, and composed a song in her praise.

JOHN C. HILL.

Girvan, Ayrshire.
6th June 1961.

Nelly Kilpatrick

1773, age 14 [1]

BURNS's first song 'My Handsome Nell' was composed when he was in the autumn of his fifteenth year.

MY HANDSOME NELL

O ONCE I lov'd a bonie lass,
    An' ay I love her still,
An' whilst that virtue warms my breast,
    I'll love my handsome Nell.

As bonie lasses I hae seèn,
    And mony full as braw,   *fine*
But, for a modest, gracefu' mien,
    The like I never saw.

A bonie lass, I will confess,
    Is pleasant to the e'e;   *eye*
But without some better qualities,
    She's no' a lass for me.

But Nelly's looks are blythe and sweet,
    And what is best of a',
Her reputation is complete,
    And fair without a flaw.

She dresses ay sae clean and neat,
    Both decent and genteel;
And then there's something in her gait
    Gars ony dress look weel.   *makes*

[1] i.e. Robert Burns's age.

I

A gaudy dress and gentle air
   May slightly touch the heart,
But it's innocence and modesty
   That polishes the dart.

'Tis this in Nelly pleases me,
   'Tis this enchants my soul,
For absolutely in my breast
   She reigns without control.

In the manuscript copy verse 4 reads:

But Nelly's looks are blythe and sweet,
   Good-humoured, frank and free;
And still the more I view them o'er,
   The more they captive me.

Nelly was the daughter of Alan Kilpatrick, the miller of Perclewan in the parish of Dalrymple, though some say he was the blacksmith at Mount Oliphant. She was Burns's partner in the labours of the harvest field gathering up the sheaves.

While at Mount Oliphant farm Burns pored over a collection of songs which was his vade-mecum as he drove his horse and cart along the country lanes. To this, he tells us, he owed his 'critic craft' such as it was. In praise of Nelly, he writes thus to Dr Moore:

'This kind of life—the cheerless gloom of a hermit, with the unceasing moil of a galley-slave—brought me to my sixteenth year; a little before which period I first committed the sin of rhyme. You know our country custom of coupling a man and woman together as partners in the labours of harvest. In my fifteenth autumn, my partner was a bewitching creature, a year younger than myself. My scarcity of English denies me the power of doing her justice in that language, but you know the Scotch idiom: she was a "bonnie, sweet, sonsie lass". In short, she, altogether unwittingly to herself, initiated me in that delicious passion which, in spite of acid disappointment, gin-horse prudence, and book-worm philosophy, I hold to be the first of human joys, our dearest blessing here below! How she caught the contagion I cannot tell; you medical people talk

BURNS COTTAGE
Alloway, Ayr
(*Page 1*)

NELLY KILPATRICK

(*Page 1*)

much of infection from breathing the same air, the touch, etc.; but I never expressly said I loved her.—Indeed, I did not know myself why I liked so much to loiter behind with her, when returning in the evening from our labours; why the tones of her voice made my heart strings thrill like an Aeolian harp; and particularly why my pulse beat such a furious ratan, when I looked and fingered over her little hand to pick out the cruel nettle-stings and thistles. Among her other love-inspiring qualities, she sang sweetly; and it was her favourite reel to which I attempted giving an embodied vehicle in rhyme. I was not so presumptuous as to imagine that I could make verses like printed ones, composed by men who had Greek and Latin; but my girl sang a song which was said to be composed by a small country laird's son, on one of his father's maids with whom he was in love; and I saw no reason why I might not rhyme as well as he; for, excepting that he could smear sheep, and cast peats, his father living in the moorlands, he had no more scholar-craft than myself. Thus with me began love and poetry.'

Although Burns refers to the song in his Commonplace Book, 1783, as 'very puerile and silly', he says: 'I am always pleased with it, as it recalls to my mind those happy days, when my heart was yet honest, and my tongue was sincere.' At another time he writes: 'It was the first of my performances, and done at an early period of my life, when my heart glowed with honest, warm simplicity,—unacquainted and uncorrupted with the ways of a wicked world. It has many faults; but I remember I composed it in a wild enthusiasm of passion; and to this hour I never recollect it but my heart melts—my blood sallies, at the remembrance.'

It may not be anything great as a song, but for pure, natural simplicity it has never been surpassed. The love it speaks of is an experience we have all known at some time or other.

Nelly married Mr William Bone, coachman to the laird of Newark, and died in 1820.

B

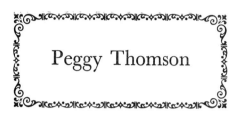

Peggy Thomson

1775–7, age 16–18

BURNS spent the last of his schooldays at Kirkoswald, a rural village about twelve miles south from Ayr. Of this period he says: 'A circumstance in my life which made some alteration in my mind and manners was, that I spent my nineteenth summer on a smuggling coast, a good distance from home, at a noted school, to learn mensuration, surveying, dialling, etc., in which I made a pretty good progress; but I made a greater progress in the knowledge of mankind. The contraband trade was at this time very successful, and it sometimes happened to me to fall in with those who carried it on. Scenes of swaggering riot and roaring dissipation were till this time quite new to me; but I was no enemy to social life. Here, though I learnt to fill my glass, and to mix without fear in a drunken squabble, yet I went on with a high hand with my geometry, till the sun entered Virgo—a month which is always a carnival in my bosom—when a charming *fillette*, who lived next door to the school, overset my trigonometry, and set me off at a tangent from the sphere of my studies. I struggled on, however, with my sines and co-sines for a few days more; but stepping into the garden one charming noon, to take the sun's altitude, there I met my angel—

> Like Proserpine gathering flowers—
> Herself a fairer flower.

It was in vain to think of doing any more good at school. The remaining week I stayed I did nothing but craze the faculties of my soul about her, or steal out to meet her. And the last two nights of my stay in the country, had sleep been a mortal sin, the

4

image of this modest and innocent girl had kept me guiltless.'
(Virgo—i.e. in August, 23.)

The charming *fillette* was Peggy Thomson. Writing later in
his Commonplace Book, April 1783, Burns says: 'If anything on
earth deserves the name of rapture or transport, it is the feelings
of green eighteen in company of the mistress of his heart, when
she repays him with an equal return of affection.'

There has always been some dubiety anent the heroine of the
song 'My Peggy's Charms', but it is now generally conceded
that it was composed in honour of Peggy Thomson.

Nothing came of the affair at the time, but several years later
in 1783, Burns renewed his acquaintance with Peggy, and from
a rough former draft, rewrote the beautiful song as follows:

My Peggy's Charms

Now westlin winds and slaught'ring guns   *western*
   Bring autumn's pleasant weather;
The moorcock springs, on whirring wings,
   Amang the blooming heather:
Now waving grain, wide o'er the plain,
   Delights the weary farmer;
And the moon shines bright, when I rove at night,
   To muse upon my charmer.

The partridge loves the fruitful fells;
   The plover loves the mountains;
The woodcock haunts the lonely dells;
   The soaring hern the fountains: *heron*
Through lofty groves the cushat roves,   *wood pigeon*
   The path of man to shun it;
The hazel bush o'erhangs the thrush,
   The spreading thorn the linnet.

Thus every kind their pleasure find,
   The savage and the tender;
Some social join, and leagues combine;
   Some solitary wander:
Avaunt, away! the cruel sway,
   Tyrannic man's dominion;
The sportsman's joy, the murdering cry,
   The fluttering, gory pinion!

But Peggy, dear, the evening's clear,
  Thick flies the skimming swallow;
The sky is blue, the fields in view,
  All fading green and yellow:
Come, let us stray our gladsome way,
  And view the charms of nature;
The rustling corn, the fruited thorn,
  And every happy creature.

We'll gently walk, and sweetly talk,
  Till the silent moon shine clearly;
I'll grasp thy waist, and, fondly prest,
  Swear how I love thee dearly:
Not vernal showers to budding flowers.
  Not autumn to the farmer,
So dear can be, as thou to me,
  My fair, my lovely charmer!

In 1784 Peggy became the wife of Mr John Neilson of Kirkoswald. In Burns's manuscript collection for Captain Riddel, 1786, the poet says: ''Twas the girl I mentioned in my letter to Dr Moore, where I speak of taking the sun's altitude. Poor Peggy! Her husband is my old acquaintance, and a most worthy fellow. When I was taking leave of my Carrick relations, intending to go to the West Indies, when I took farewell of her, neither she nor I could speak a syllable. Her husband escorted me three miles on my road, and we both parted with tears.'

Before saying goodbye to Peggy, Burns presented her with a first edition of his poems, with the following lines written on the blank leaf:

Once fondly lov'd, and still remember'd dear,
  Sweet early object of my youthful vows,
Accept this mark of friendship, warm, sincere—
  Friendship! 'tis all cold duty now allows:—
And when you read the simple, artless rhymes,
  One friendly sigh for him—he asks no more—
Who distant burns in flaming torrid climes,
  Or haply lies beneath th' Atlantic roar.

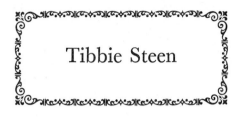

Tibbie Steen

1776, age 17

TIBBIE STEEN—her local name—was Miss Isabella Steven. She was the daughter of a farmer at Little Hill, which adjoined Lochlea, where Burns lived. It is said that his three acres of land were really nothing but peat moss!

Tibbie was regarded as a beautiful young lady and there is no doubt Burns was in love with her. He would be about seventeen years of age at this time and 'deemed himself doing well in his courtship', until she came into a legacy and tocher of £75. She now considered herself above his station of life, and sought another lover better placed than that of a poor ploughman. On visiting her house one evening he was politely informed that Tibbie was not available as she was engaged with another admirer. Burns at once turned on his heel, and never went back again to see her. She got married soon after to this other suitor, but Burns did not forget her. He composed a caustic, depreciatory song, and it is by it alone that Tibbie is remembered. She lived, however, to see the day when she was proud to acknowledge that she had once possessed the affections of the poet, and to tell her grandson, when he recited the song, that she herself was the heroine of it.

O TIBBIE, I HAE SEEN THE DAY

CHORUS

O Tibbie, I hae seen the day,   have
   Ye would na been sae shy,   would not have
For lack o' gear ye lightly me,   riches; scorn
   But, trowth, I care na by.   truth; care not although
                                     you do

7

YESTREEN I met ye on the moor,   *last night*
Ye spak na, but gaed by like stoure;   *spoke not; blowing dust*
Ye geck at me because I'm poor,   *toss the head*
   But fient a hair care I!   *fiend*
     O *Tibbie, I hae*, etc.

I doubt na, lass, but ye may think,
Because ye hae the name o' clink,   *money*
That ye can please me at a wink,
   Whene'er ye like to try.
     O *Tibbie, I hae*, etc.

But sorrow tak' him that's sae mean,
Altho' his pouch o' coin were clean,
Wha follows ony saucy quean
   That looks sae proud and high.
     O *Tibbie, I hae*, etc.

Altho' a lad were e'er sae smart;
If that he want the yellow dirt,
Ye'll cast your head anither airt,   *direction*
   And answer him fu' dry.
     O *Tibbie, I hae*, etc.

But if he hae the name o' gear,
Ye'll fasten to him like a brier;
Tho' hardly he for sense or lear   *learning*
   Be better than the kye.   *cows*
     O *Tibbie, I hae*, etc.

But, Tibbie, lass, tak my advice:
Your daddie's gear maks you sae nice;
The deil a ane wad speir your price,   *ask*
   Were ye as poor as I.
     O *Tibbie, I hae*, etc.

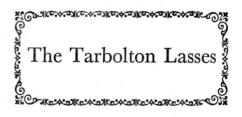

The Tarbolton Lasses

1777, age 18

BURNS composed songs on most of the handsome girls in Tarbolton, and finally the following popular song to embrace them all:

GREEN GROW THE RASHES

CHORUS

Green grow the rashes, O;   rushes
Green grow the rashes, O;
The sweetest hours that e'er I spent
Were spent amang the lasses, O.

THERE's nought but care on ev'ry han',
   In ev'ry hour that passes, O:
What signifies the life o' man,
   An' 'twere na for the lasses, O.
     Green grow, etc.

The warl'y race may riches chase,   *worldly*
   An' riches still may fly them, O;
An' tho' at last they catch them fast,
   Their hearts can ne'er enjoy them, O.
     Green grow, etc.

But gie me a canny hour at e'en,   *quiet; evening*
   My arms about my Dearie, O;
An' warl'y cares, an' warl'y men,
   May a' gae tapsalteerie, O!   *topsyturvy*
     Green grow, etc.

9

For you sae douse, wha sneer at this,   *prudent*
   Ye're nought but senseless asses, O:
The wisest Man the warl' e'er saw,
   He dearly lov'd the lasses, O.
     Green grow, etc.

Auld Nature swears, the lovely Dears
   Her noblest work she classes, O,
Her prentice han' she try'd on man,
   An' then she made the lasses, O.
     Green grow, etc.

'This song', says Burns, 'is the genuine language of my heart, and will enable anybody to determine which of the classes—the grave or the merry—I belong to.' 'My heart', he says, in a letter to Dr Moore, 'was completely tinder, and was eternally lighted up by some goddess or another . . . At plough, scythe, or reap-hook I feared no competitor, and thus I set absolute want at defiance; and as I never cared further for my labours than while I was in actual exercise, I spent the evenings in the way after my own heart. A country lad seldom carries on a love adventure without an assistant confidant. I possessed a curiosity, zeal, and intrepid dexterity that recommended me as a proper second on these occasions; and I daresay I felt as much pleasure in being in the secret of half the loves of the parish of Tarbolton, as ever did statesman in knowing the intrigues of half the courts of Europe. The grave sons of science, ambition, or avarice, baptize these things by the name of follies; but to the sons and daughters of labour and poverty, they are matters of the most serious nature. To them the ardent hope, the stolen interview, the tender farewell, are the greatest and most delicious parts of their enjoyments.'

Burns would never risk a rebuff from any young lady he proposed to court. He accordingly had a second or abettor in one or other of his numerous loves. In Tarbolton his second was a young man called John Lees. At night-time they would go to the houses where the girls lived or down to the dance hall, and while Burns waited outside or sat in the public-house bar, John would approach the selected girl and ask her if she would like to meet Robert Burns of Mossgiel, who happened to be outside.

On her agreeing, he would conduct her outside and introduce
her to the poet, when Burns would say to him: 'Now, Jock, you
may gang hame!'

THE TARBOLTON LASSES

IF ye gae up to yon hill-tap,	*go*
Ye'll there see bonie Peggy;	*pretty*
She kens her father is a laird,	
And she forsooth's a leddy.	*lady*

There Sophy tight, a lassie bright,   *strong*
    Besides a handsome fortune:
Wha canna win her in a night,
    Has little art in courting.

Gae down by Faile, and taste the ale,   *go*
    And tak' a look o' Mysie;
She's dour and din, a deil within,   *sulky; sallow*
    But aiblins she may please ye.   *perhaps*

If she be shy, her sister try,
    Ye'll maybe fancy Jenny,
If ye'll dispense wi' want o' sense—
    She kens hersel' she's bonie.   *knows; hand-*
          some

And should ye ride by yon hill-side,
    Speer in for bonie Bessy;   *call in*
She'll gie ye a beck, and bid ye light,   *a curtsy*
    And handsomely address ye.

There's few sae bonie, nane sae gude, *so good*
    In a' King George' dominion;
The truth o' this ye needna doubt—
    It's Bessy's ain opinion!   *own*

Burns's tall, athletic frame, his haughty, swarthy countenance
lit by his dark, glowing eyes, his winning tongue and deferential
manner, says his brother Gilbert, must have won him favour
among the lasses of Tarbolton, but they had enough of worldly
wisdom to deny the suit of one whose possession in life was so

little assured as the ploughman poet's was. He would fain have
offered heart and hand to Annie Ronald, but again he feared a
summary dismissal, and contented himself with celebrating his
timid passion with verse.

THE RONALDS OF THE BENNALS
1778, age 19

In Tarbolton, ye ken, there are proper young men,   *know*
   And proper young lasses and a', man;
But ken ye the Ronalds that live in the Bennals,
   They carry the gree frae them a', man.   *palm*

Their father's a laird, and weel he can spare 't,   *well*
   Braid money to tocher them a', man,   *broad; dower*
To proper young men, he'll clink in the hand
   Gowd guineas a hunder or twa, man.   *gold*

There's ane they ca' Jean, I'll warrant ye've seen
   As bonnie a lass or as braw, man;   *well dressed*
But for sense and guid taste she'll vie wi' the best,
   And a conduct that beautifies a', man.

The charms o' the min', the langer they shine,   *mind*
   The mair admiration they draw, man;
While peaches and cherries, and roses and lilies,
   They fade and they wither awa', man.

If ye be for Miss Jean, tak' this frae a frien',
   A hint o' a rival or twa, man,
The Laird o' Blackbyre wad gang through the fire,   *would go*
   If that wad entice her awa', man.   *away*

The Laird o' Braehead has been on his speed,
   For mair than a towmond or twa, man,   *twelve-month*
The Laird o' the Ford will straught on a board   *be stretched in*
   If he canna get her at a', man.   *death*

Then Annie comes in, the pride o' her kin,
   The boast of our bachelors a', man:
Sae sonsy and sweet, sae fully complete,   *so buxom*
   She steals our affections awa', man.

If I should detail the pick and the wale   *choice*
  O' lasses that live here awa', man,
The fault wad be mine, if she didna shine,
  The sweetest and best o' them a', man.

I lo'e her mysel', but darena weel tell,
  My poverty keeps me in awe, man,
For making o' rhymes, and working at times,
  Does little or naething at a', man.

Yet I wadna choose to let her refuse,   *would not*
  Nor hae't in her power to say na, man,
For though I be poor, unnoticed, obscure,
  My stomach's as proud as them a', man.

Though I canna ride in weel-booted pride,
  And flee o'er the hills like a craw, man,   *crow*
I can haud up my head wi' the best o' the breed, *hold*
  Though fluttering ever so braw, man.   *brave*

My coat and my vest, they are Scotch o' the best,
  O' pairs o' gude breeks I hae twa, man,   *breeches*
And stockings and pumps to put on my stumps, *legs*
  And ne'er a wrang steek in them a', man.   *stitch*

My sarks they are few, but five o' them new,   *shirts*
  Twal'-hundred, as white as the snaw, man,
A ten-shillings hat, a Holland cravat;
  There are no' mony poets sae braw, man.   *handsome*

I never had frien's, weel stockit in means,
  To leave me a hundred or twa, man,
Nae weel-tochered aunts, to wait on their drants, *dowered;* *drawls*
  And wish them in hell for it a', man.   [—*long prayers*

I never was canny for hoarding o' money,   *careful*
  Or claughtin't together at a', man   *grasping*
I've little to spend, and naething to lend,
  But deevil a shilling I awe, man.   *owe*

The two young ladies were spoken of as the predominant
belles of the district. Their father was wealthy, and encouraged

the poet, but Jean said she 'couldna' see aught aboot Rabbie
Burns that would tempt her tae sit up till twal o'clock at night
wi' him!' She carried on a lengthy correspondence with Gilbert
Burns, but in the end refused him on the ground of his poverty.

ADVICE TO LOVE-SICK LADS
Oh, Steer Her Up

Oh, steer her up and haud her gaun—	*rouse; keep her going*
Her mither's at the mill, jo;	*love*
And gin she winna tak a man	*if; will not*
E'en let her tak her will, jo:	
First shore her wi' a kindly kiss.	*entice*
And ca' anither gill, jo;	
And gin she tak the thing amiss,	*should she*
E'en let her flyte her fill, jo.	*scold*
Oh, steer her up, and be na blate,	*not bashful*
And gin she tak it ill, jo,	
Then lea'e the lassie till her fate,	*leave; to*
And time nae langer spill, jo:	*waste*
Ne'er break your heart for ae rebute,	*one rebuff*
But think upon it still, jo;	
That gin the lassie winna do 't,	
Ye 'll fin' anither will, jo.	*find*

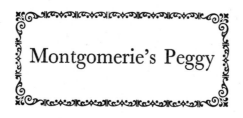

MONTGOMERIE'S PEGGY

ALTHO' my bed were in yon muir   *moor*
  Amang the heather, in my plaidie,
Yet happy, happy would I be,
  Had I my dear Montgomerie's Peggy.

When o'er the hill beat surly storms,
  And winter nights were dark and rainy,
I'd seek some dell, and in my arms
  I'd shelter dear Montgomerie's Peggy.

Were I a Baron proud and high,
  And horse and servants waiting ready,
Then a' 'twad gie o' joy to me,   *all it would give*
  The sharin't wi' Montgomerie's Peggy. *sharing it*

BURNS was only a short time at Lochlea when he found his way, along with other lads, to see the maids at Coilsfield House, the Castle of Montgomerie. Soon he became a favourite and laid siege to the heart of the housekeeper, his 'Montgomerie's Peggy'.

In his Commonplace Book, 1785, he says: 'My Montgomerie's Peggy was my deity for six or eight months. She had been bred in a style of life rather elegant. But, as Vanbrugh says in one of his comedies, my 'damn'd star found me out', there too; for, though I began the affair merely in a *gaieté de cœur*, or, to tell the truth, what would scarcely be believed, a vanity of showing my parts in courtship, particularly my abilities at a *billet-doux* (which I always piqued myself upon), made me lay siege to her; and when, as I always do in my foolish gallantries, I had battered myself into a very warm affection for her, she told me one day in a flag of truce, that her fortress had been for some time before the rightful property of another, but with the greatest friendship and politeness, she offered me every alliance except actual possession. I found out afterwards that what she told me of a pre-engagement was really true; but it cost me some heart Achs to get rid of the affair.'

Some confusion has arisen between Ellison Begbie and Montgomerie's Peggy, but Agnes Begg, the poet's sister, has made it quite clear that Ellison was not Peggy.

'How Mr D. runs into the mistake of saying that Mrs Begg, in her account of Ellison Begbie, represented her as the same with "Montgomerie's Peggy", is to me incomprehensible. She has ever said the very reverse; for they were as distinct as two women with two souls can be. "Montgomerie's Peggy" was housekeeper at Coilsfield, not to Colonel Montgomery, but to his father, A. Montgomery, Esq. The poet and she had met frequently at Tarboth Mill (the "Willie's Mill" of Dr Hornbook); they sat in the same church, and had had a good deal of intercourse; but she was engaged to another before ever they met; so, on her part, it was nothing but amusement, and on Burns's part, little else, from the way he speaks of it.' (Agnes Begg.)

Despite what Mrs Begg says, I think Burns was really in deep love with Peggy, and that his offer to her of marriage was genuine. The other lover, however, was successful, and soon after parting with the disconsolate Burns she got married.

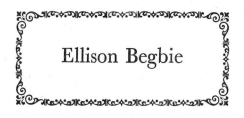

Ellison Begbie

1780, age 21

BUT it's not her air, her form, her face,
    Though matching beauty's fabled queen;
'Tis the mind that shines in every grace;
    And chiefly in her *roguish* een.

'ALL these charming qualities, heightened by an education much beyond anything I have ever met in any woman I ever dared to approach, have made an impression on my heart that I do not think the world can ever efface.' (Letter to E. B., 1780.)

These glowing words refer to Ellison Begbie, who was the daughter of a small farmer in the parish of Galston. Apparently her services were not required at home, so that she became a serving-maid to a family at Cessnock in the neighbourhood of Lochlea. Burns praised 'her uncommon personal advantages, her superior education and good sense, her amiable goodness, tender feminine softness, endearing sweetness of disposition, with all the charming offspring of a warm, feeling heart'. Surely an angelic young woman!

Burns wrote at least four letters to her during 1780-1 in which he expressed the most ardent love for her and sincerely hoped to make her his wife and to settle down. And an excellent wife she would have made to the poet. How passionately fond of her he was is apparent in his song to her:

17

An' I'll Kiss thee Yet

CHORUS

An' I'll kiss thee yet, yet,
An' I'll kiss thee o'er again;
An' I'll kiss thee yet, yet,
My bonie Peggy Alison.

WHEN in my arms, wi' a' thy charms,
　I clasp my countless treasure, O!
I seek nae mair o' Heav'n to share,　　*no more*
　Than sic a moment's pleasure, O!　　*such*

Ilk care and fear, when thou art near,
　I ever mair defy them, O!
Young kings upon their hansel throne
　Are nae sae blest as I am, O!

And by thy een sae bonie blue,　　*eyes*
　I swear I'm thine for ever, O!
And on thy lips I seal my vow,
　And break it shall I never, O!

The name Ellison Begbie did not lend itself easily to rhyme, so Burns frequently adopted cognomens such as in the chorus of this song when he calls her by the surname 'Alison'.

This was confirmed by Mrs Begg.

The next song was recovered by Cromek from the oral communication of a lady in Glasgow, whom the bard early in life affectionately admired. He adds that it is an early production. It contains more of simile than of passion. The young poet was perhaps anxious to display his ingenuity in likening the object of his affection to the most pleasing objects in nature: he called to mind the freshness of the morning dawn, the twinkling of the dew-drop upon the lawn, the fragrant breeze of evening gently stirring the blossomed bean, the stateliness of the young ash, the spotless purity of the flowering hawthorn and the sweet notes of the thrush as he cheers his mate with his evening song; and to each of these he found a corresponding quality in the lass of Cessnock Banks.

TIBBIE STEEN
(*Page 7*)

JEAN ARMOUR MEETING BURNS

(*Page 32*)

The Lass of Cessnock Banks

A SONG OF SIMILES

On Cessnock banks a lassie dwells;
　　Could I describe her shape and mien;
Our lasses a' she far excels,
　　An' she has twa sparkling, roguish een.　　*eyes*

She's sweeter than the morning dawn
　　When rising Phoebus first is seen,
And dew-drops twinkle o'er the lawn,—
　　An' she has twa sparkling, roguish een.

She's stately, like yon youthful ash
　　That grows the cowslip braes between,
And drinks the stream with vigour fresh,—
　　An' she has twa sparkling, roguish een.

She's spotless, like the flow'ring thorn
　　With flow'rs so white and leaves so green,
When purest in the dewy morn,—
　　An' she has twa sparkling, roguish een.

Her looks are like the vernal May,
　　When ev'ning Phoebus shines serene,
While birds rejoice on every spray,—
　　An' she has twa sparkling, roguish een.

Her hair is like the curling mist
　　That climbs the mountain-sides at e'en,
When flow'r-reviving rains are past,—
　　An' she has twa sparkling, roguish een.

Her forehead's like the show'ry bow
　　When gleaming sunbeams intervene,
And gild the distant mountain's brow,—
　　An' she has twa sparkling, roguish een.

Her cheeks are like yon crimson gem,
　　The pride of all the flowery scene,
Just opening on its thorny stem,—
　　An' she has twa sparkling, roguish een.

C

Her lips are like yon cherries ripe,
   That sunny walls from Boreas screen;
They tempt the taste and charm the sight,—
   An' she has twa sparkling, roguish een.

Her teeth are like the nightly snow
   When pale the morning rises keen,
While hid the murm'ring streamlets flow;
   An' she has twa sparkling, roguish een.

Her breath is like the fragrant breeze
   That gently stirs the blossom'd bean,
When Phoebus sinks behind the seas;
   An' she has twa sparkling, roguish een.

Her voice is like the ev'ning thrush
   That sings on Cessnock banks unseen,
While his mate sits nestling in the bush;
   An' she has twa sparkling, roguish een.

But it's not her air, her form, her face,
   Tho' matching beauty's fabled queen,
'Tis the mind that shines in ev'ry grace,
   An' chiefly in her roguish een.

In his last letter to her Burns declared that the part he was playing was worthy of a man and of a Christian, and if she would be so good and so generous as to admit him for her partner, her companion and her bosom friend through life, nothing on this side of eternity would give him greater transport.

Ellison, however, in the politest language of refusal wrote that she was very sorry she could not make him a return, but wished him all kind of happiness. Soon after she was married to another suitor.

For several months Burns suffered much in spirit over this disappointment, feeling that Ellison had not treated him in an honourable fashion. Writing to Dr Moore, he says: 'The clouds of misfortune were gathering thick round my father's head; the darkest of which was—he was visibly far gone in a consumption. To crown all, a *belle fille* whom I adored, and who had pledged her soul to meet me in the fields of matrimony, jilted me, with peculiar circumstances of mortification.'

The reference here, says Mrs Begg, is to Ellison Begbie. It is only fair to say, however, that in later years Ellison declared that she had never at any time agreed to any proposal of marriage made by Burns.

The impression left by Ellison upon the poet's mind, however, was not eradicated, for many years afterwards we find him confessing that, of all women he had ever courted, he had met with no one who could have made such a companion for life as Ellison Begbie. Upon which declaration James Hogg, the Ettrick Shepherd, in his own quaint way remarks: 'There is no doubt hanging and marriage go by destiny, else Burns should have had this sensible girl.'

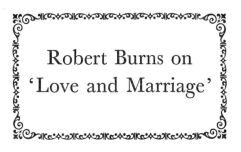

Robert Burns on 'Love and Marriage'

My Dear E——,

I do not remember, in the course of your acquaintance and mine, ever to have heard your opinion on the ordinary way of falling in love amongst people in our station in life; I do not mean the persons who proceed in the way of bargain, but those whose affection is really placed on the person.

Though I be, as you know very well, but a very awkward lover myself, yet, as I have some opportunities of observing the conduct of others who are much better skilled in the affair of courtship than I am, I often think it is owing to lucky chance, more than to good management, that there are not more unhappy marriages than usually are.

It is natural for a young fellow to like the acquaintance of the females, and customary for him to keep them company when occasion serves; some one of them is more agreeable to him than the rest; there is something, he knows not what, pleases him, he knows not how, in her company. This I take to be what is called love with the greater part of us; and I must own, my dear Eliza, it is a hard game such a one as you have to play when you meet with such a lover. You cannot refuse but he is sincere; and yet though you use him ever so favourably, perhaps in a few months, or at furthest in a year or two, the same unaccountable fancy may make him as distractedly fond of another, whilst you are quite forgot. I am aware that perhaps the next time I have the pleasure of seeing you, you may bid me take my own lesson home, and tell me that the passion I have professed for you is perhaps one of those transient flashes I have been describing; but I hope, my dear Eliza, you will do me the justice to believe me, when I assure you that the love I have for you is founded on the sacred principles of virtue and honour, and by consequence so long as you continue possessed of those amiable qualities which first inspired my passion for you, so long must I continue to love you. Believe me, my dear, it is love like this alone which can render the marriage state happy. People may talk of flames and raptures as long as they please, and a warm fancy, with a flow of youthful spirits, may make them feel something like what they describe; but sure I am the nobler faculties of the mind with kindred feelings of the heart can only be the foundation of friendship, and it has always been my opinion that the married life was only friendship in a more exalted degree. If you will be so good as to grant my wishes, and it should please Providence to spare us to the latest period of life, I can look forward and see that even then, though bent down with wrinkled age,—even then, when all other worldly circumstances will be indifferent to me, I will regard my Eliza with the tenderest affection, and for this plain reason, because she is still possessed of these noble qualities, improved to a much higher degree, which first inspired my affection for her.

> Oh happy state when souls each other draw
> Where love is liberty and nature law!

I know were I to speak in such a style to many a girl who thinks herself possessed of no small share of sense, she would think it ridiculous; but the language of the heart is, my dear Eliza, the only courtship I shall ever use to you.

When I look over what I have written, I am sensible it is vastly different from the ordinary style of courtship; but I shall make no apology—I know your good-nature will excuse what your good sense may see amiss.

R. B.

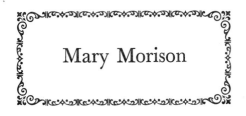

Mary Morison

1780, age 21

MARY MORISON

O MARY, at thy window be,
 It is the wish'd, the trysted hour;
Those smiles and glances let me see,
 That make the miser's treasure poor:
How blythely wad I bide the stoure, *bear the toil*
 A weary slave frae sun to sun;
Could I the rich reward secure—
 The lovely Mary Morison!

Yestreen, when to the trembling string, *yesternight*
 The dance gaed thro' the lighted ha', *went; hall*
To thee my fancy took its wing,
 I sat, but neither heard nor saw:
Tho' this was fair, and that was braw, *handsome*
 And yon the toast of a' the town,
I sigh'd, and said amang them a',
 'Ye are na Mary Morison.' *not*

O Mary, canst thou wreck his peace,
 Wha for thy sake wad gladly dee? *die*
Or canst thou break that heart of his,
 Whase only faut is loving thee? *fault*
If love for love thou wilt na gie, *not give*
 At least be pity to me shown;
A thought ungentle canna be *cannot*
 The thought o' Mary Morison.

IN A LETTER to Mr G. Thomson, 20th March 1793, Burns
says: 'My Dear Sir,—The song prefixed ("Mary Morison") is

one of my juvenile works. I leave it in your hands. I do not think it very remarkable, either for its merits or demerits.'

This judgment, however, is not the verdict of history. William Hazlitt speaks for modern times when he says: 'Of all the productions of Burns, the pathetic and serious love-songs which he has left behind him, in the manner of old ballads, are perhaps those which take the deepest and most lasting hold of the mind. Such are the lines to "Mary Morison".'

Mary was the daughter of Adjutant Morison, well known and respected in Mauchline, and Burns first met her at the tea-table of a friend. In Mauchline churchyard there is a tombstone erected in 1825 with the inscription:

'In memory of Adj. John Morison, of the 104th Regt., who died at Mauchline, 16 April, 1804, in the 86th year of his age. Also his daughter, Mary, the Poet's bonnie Mary Morison, who died 29 June, 1791, aged 20, and his second spouse, Ann Tomlinson, who died 6 Sep., 1831, aged 76.'

The Rev. Dr Edgar, minister at Mauchline, in his book *Old Church Life in Scotland* says: 'I am informed, on authority, that a member of the adjutant's family, who lived to be a grandmother, used to speak of Burns (with aversion, I may add) as one whom she knew personally, when he lived at Mauchline, and that, she believed her sister Mary was the "lovely Mary Morison" whom the poet admired. She often spoke of this long-lost Mary, who died in early youth, from the amputation of a foot that had been accidentally injured, as "one of the fairest creatures the sun ever shone upon".'

The song is deservedly popular, breathing as it does an atmosphere of pure love and devotion.

Some writers have conjectured that the song refers to Ellison Begbie, but this is unlikely, as Burns would have used in that case the name he used in song for her, namely Peggy Alison, which *rhymes quite as well* as Mary Morison.

Agnes Fleming

1781, age 22

('Nannie')

Behind yon hills, where Lugar flows
  'Mang moors and mosses many, O,   *bogs*
The wintry sun the day has closed,
  And I'll awa' to Nannie, O.

The westlin wind blaws loud and shrill: *western*
  The night's baith mirk and rainy, O;   *dark*
But I'll get my plaid, and out I'll steal.
  And owre the hills to Nannie, O.   *over*

My Nannie's charming, sweet, and young,
  Nae artfu' wiles to win ye, O:
May ill befa' the flattering tongue
  That wad beguile my Nannie, O.   *would*

Her face is fair, her heart is true,
  As spotless as she's bonie, O:
The opening gowan, wat wi' dew,   *wet*
  Nae purer is than Nannie, O.

A country lad is my degree,
  And few there be that ken me, O:
But what care I how few they be,
  I'm welcome aye to Nannie, O.

My riches a's my penny-fee,   *wages*   [*fully*
   And I maun guide it cannie, O;   *I must; gentle, care-*
But warl's gear ne'er troubles me,   *worldly wealth*
   My thoughts are a' my Nannie, O.

Our auld guidman delights to view
   His sheep and kye thrive bonie, O;   *cows*
But I'm as blythe that hauds his pleugh,   *holds*
   And has na care but Nannie, O.

Come weel, come woe, I care na by,
   I'll tak what Heav'n will send me, O;
Nae ither care in life have I,   *no other*
   But live, an' love my Nannie, O.

AGNES FLEMING was the daughter of a farmer at Coldcothill, half a mile north of Lochlea in the parish of Tarbolton. She was for some time a serving-maid in the house of Gavin Hamilton, Burns's friend in Mauchline.

Writing about Agnes in 1819, the Rev. Hamilton Paul, one of the contemporaries of Burns, says:

'In Kilmarnock Burns first saw Nannie the subject of one of his most popular ballads. She captivated him as well by the charms of her person as by the melody of her voice. As he devoted much of his spare time to her society, and listened to her singing with the most religious attention, her sister observed to him that he paid more attention to Nannie's singing than he would do to a preaching, and he retorted, with an oath: "Madam, there's no comparison."'

However, I am rather inclined to agree with Gilbert Burns, who held that the poet first saw Nannie in Tarbolton.

Be that as it may, Burns says in his Commonplace Book in 1784: 'As I have been all along a miserable dupe in Love, and have been led into a thousand weaknesses and follies by it, for that reason I put the more confidence in my critical skill in distinguishing foppery and conceit from real passion and nature. Whether the following song will stand the test, I will not pretend to say, because it is my own; only, I can say, it was, at the time, real.'

In the song Burns 'flitted' Nannie in imagination first to the

Stincher and then to the Lugar, that the 'charming, sweet, and young creature might be connected with a sweeter sound'.

It is gratifying to know that Burns's father lived to read this song and that he expressed his hearty admiration of it, as also did the people of Tarbolton and Mauchline.

Agnes died unmarried at an advanced age—'surely', as one Burns enthusiast says, 'no fit destiny for one who had been the subject of such a strain!'

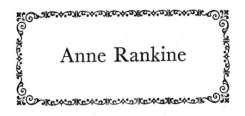

1782, age 23

THE RIGS O' BARLEY

It was upon a Lammas night,
 When corn rigs are bonie, O,   *ridges*
Beneath the moon's unclouded light
 I held awa to Annie, O;
The time flew by, wi' tentless heed, *careless*
 Till 'tween the late and early, O, *dark and dawn*
Wi' sma' persuasion she agreed,
 To see me thro' the barley, O.

CHORUS

Corn rigs, an' barley rigs,
 An' corn rigs are bonie, O,
O, I'll ne'er forget that happy night,
 Amang the rigs wi' Annie, O.

The sky was blue, the wind was still,
 The moon was shining clearly, O,
I set her down, wi' right good will,
 Amang the rigs o' barley, O:
I ken't her heart was a' my ain; *knew; own*
 I lov'd her most sincerely, O:
I kiss'd her owre and owre again, *over*
 Amang the rigs o' barley, O.

I lock'd her in my fond embrace;
 Her heart was beating rarely, O:
My blessings on that happy place,
 Amang the rigs o' barley, O!

But by the moon and stars so bright,
  That shone that night so clearly, O!
She ay shall bless that happy night,
  Amang the rigs o' barley, O!

I hae been blythe wi' Comrades dear;
  I hae been merry drinking, O:
I hae been joyfu' gath'rin' gear;   *money*
  I hae been happy thinking, O:
But a' the pleasures e'er I saw,
  Tho' three times doubl'd fairly, O,
That happy night was worth them a',
  Amang the rigs o' barley, O.

THE ABOVE song is one of Burns's early productions. It breathes the simplicity of youth, the beauty of the natural scene and is deservedly popular.

Chambers states that Anne Rankine always declared that she was the 'Annie' of the song. She remembered the incident well; 'when', she said, 'I was a fair young lassie amang the rigs o' barley'. After the publication of the song in 1782, meeting Burns one day she told him that she little expected to be celebrated in print, to which he replied: 'Oh ay, I was just wanting to give you a cast among the lave!'

Anne was the youngest daughter of John Rankine, farmer of Adamhill, two miles or so from Lochlea. She married Mr John Merry, an innkeeper in Cumnock. He died in 1802 and thereafter she kept the inn herself.

Burns was passionately fond of her, and made her a present of a lock of his hair and one of his miniature likenesses, which Anne treasured along with the song all her life.

She died in 1843 and was buried in Cumnock old churchyard.

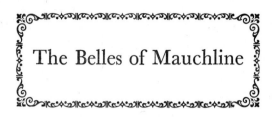

The Belles of Mauchline

1784, age 25

In Mauchline there dwells six proper young belles,
  The pride o' the place and its neighbourhood a';
Their carriage and dress, a stranger would guess,
  In Lon'on or Paris they'd gotten it a':

Miss Miller is fine, *Miss Markland*'s divine,
  Miss Smith she has wit, and *Miss Betty* is braw;   *beautifully dressed*
There's beauty and fortune to get wi' *Miss Morton*;
  But *Armour*'s the jewel for me o' them a'.

The 'Six Belles' were: The fine Miss Helen Miller who married
Burns's great friend, Dr Mackenzie; the divine Miss Markland
who married James Finlay, an excise officer, another friend of
Burns; witty Jean Smith who married yet another friend, James
Candlish, and was the mother of the great scholar and preacher,
Dr Robert S. Candlish of Edinburgh; braw Betty Miller, sister
of Miss Helen Miller, who became Mrs Templeton; and Miss
Morton gave her beauty and fortune to Mr Paterson, a Mauch-
line merchant; while Jean Armour, 'the jewel o' them a'', was
wedded to Robert Burns, the ploughman poet.

Jean Armour
(Bonie Jean)

1784–1796

Not vernal showers to budding flowers, not Autumn to the farmer,
So dear can be as thou to me, my bonie Jeanie Armour.

I LOVE MY JEAN

OF a' the airts the wind can blaw,   *directions*
  I dearly lo'e the west;
For there the bonie lassie lives,
  The lassie I lo'e best:
There wild-woods grow, and rivers row,   *roll*
  And mony a hill between;
But, day and night, my fancy's flight
  Is ever wi' my Jean.

I see her in the dewy flowers,
  I see her sweet and fair;
I hear her in the tunefu' birds,
  Wi' music charm the air:
There's not a bonie flower that springs
  By fountain, shaw, or green;
There's not a bonie bird that sings,
  But minds me o' my Jean.

'I COMPOSED this song', says Burns, 'out of compliment to Mrs Burns during our honeymoon.' While he was busy preparing Ellisland for her, she remained at Mossgiel. Hence the expression 'I dearly lo'e the west', for in summer, seen from Ellisland, the sun sets in the direction of Mossgiel.

Jean Armour was the daughter of a master-mason and con-
tractor in Mauchline, and was born 27th February 1767. There
is an interesting story told of the first meeting between Burns
and Jean. Towards the end of April there was a race at Mauchline, when the custom was for the young men of the village to
invite local girls to Hugh Morton's ballroom, which occupied
the second flat of a public house next door to Mauchline Castle.

The poet was followed into the hall by his dog, which caused
some amusement as well as confusion among the dancers, by
following his master all over the floor, and Burns remarked in
jocular fashion to his partner (not Jean) that he wished some
lassie would like him as well as his dog did.

Jean, dancing alongside with another partner, overheard the
remark, and she recalled it when some days later as she was
bleaching clothes on Mauchline green, Burns's dog ran among
them as his master was passing through the village, and she
called on the poet to whistle his dog off. During the conversation
which ensued, Jean, remembering the episode at the dance,
playfully asked if Burns had yet got any of the lassies to like him
as well as his dog did.

Thus began the romance between Burns and Bonie Jean.

THE MAUCHLINE LADY

WHEN first I came to Stewart Kyle,
  My mind it was na steady;
Where'er I gaed, where'er I rade,   *went; rode*
  A mistress still I had aye:
But when I came roun' by Mauchline town,
  Not dreadin' onie body,   *any*
My heart was caught before I thought—
  And by a Mauchline lady.

Jean won the chief place in his affections but their relation-
ship proved so unfortunate that in 1786 a secret and irregular
marriage with a written acknowledgment of it had to be
effected, and shortly afterwards she became the mother of twin
children. Her father's indignation was great over the downfall
of his daughter, and such was his hatred towards the father of

her children that he compelled her to destroy the document which vouched for her marriage with Burns. The poet himself seems not to have looked upon his marriage as legal for, two years afterwards, the opposition from his wife's family having been withdrawn, he had the ceremony regularly performed and forthwith acknowledged Jean Armour as his wife.

Writing to Peggy Chalmers, 16th September 1788, Burns says: 'Shortly after my last return to Ayrshire, I married "my Jean". This was not in consequence of the attachment of romance, perhaps; but I had a long and much-loved fellow-creature's happiness or misery in my determination, and I durst not trifle with so important a deposit. Nor have I any cause to repent it. If I have not got polite tattle, modish manners, and fashionable dress, I am not sickened and disgusted with the multiform curse of boarding-school affectation: and I have got the handsomest figure, the sweetest temper, the soundest constitution, and the kindest heart in the county. Mrs Burns believes, as firmly as her creed, that I am *le plus bel esprit, et le plus honnête homme* in the universe; although she scarcely ever in her life, except the Scriptures of the Old and the New Testament, and the Psalms of David in metre, spent five minutes together on either prose or verse. I must except also from this last a certain late publication of Scots poems, which she has perused very devoutly; and all the ballads in the country, as she has (O the partial lover! you will cry) the finest "wood note wild" I ever heard. I am the more particular in this lady's character, as I know she will henceforth have the honour of a share in your best wishes. She is still at Mauchline.'

In his 'Epistle to Davie, a Brother Poet', Burns says:

> Ye hae your MEG, your dearest part,
> And I my darling JEAN!
> It warms me, it charms me,
> To mention but her *name*:
> It heats me, it beats me,
> And sets me a' on flame!

Bonie Jean knew full well that she was not the only woman that Burns had ever loved nor the first one he had asked to marry

JEAN ARMOUR
'Bonie Jean'
(*Page 37*)

THE LASS O' BALLOCHMYLE
Wilhelmina Alexander
(*Page 48*)

him. She knew that after the death of 'Highland Mary' he wrote some lovely lyrics to his 'dear departed shade', but she understood him and knew that his love for her in his heart was in no way affected.

It is na, Jean, thy Bonie Face

It is na, Jean, thy bonie face   *not*
    Nor shape that I admire;
Altho' thy beauty and thy grace,
    Might weel awauk desire: *well awake*
Something, in ilka part o' thee,   *every*
    To praise, to love, I find;
But dear as is thy form to me,
    Still dearer is thy mind.

Nae mair ungen'rous wish I hae,   *no more; have*
    Nor stronger in my breast,
Than, if I canna mak thee sae,   *so*
    At least to see thee blest.
Content am I, if Heaven shall give
    But happiness to thee:
And as wi' thee I'd wish to live,
    For thee I'd bear to dee.

When he was contemplating the voyage to the West Indies he wrote the following sweet snatch:

My Jean

Though cruel fate should bid us part,
    Far as the pole and line,
Her dear idea round my heart
    Should tenderly entwine.
Though mountains rise, and deserts howl.
    And oceans roar between;
Yet, dearer than my deathless soul,
    I still would love my Jean.

Lockhart, in his *Life of Burns*, says: 'He brought his wife home to Ellisland about the end of November (1788); and few housekeepers start with a larger provision of young mouths to feed that did this couple. Mrs Burns had lain-in this autumn, for the

D

second time, of twins, and I suppose "sonsy, smirking, dear-bought Bess", accompanied her younger brothers and sisters from Mossgiel. From that quarter also Burns brought a whole establishment of servants, male and female, who, of course, as was then the universal custom amongst the small farmers, both of the west and of the south of Scotland, partook at the same table of the same fare with their master and mistress. Ellisland is beautifully situated on the banks of the Nith, about six miles above Dumfries, exactly opposite to the house of Dalswinton, and those noble woods and gardens amidst which Burns's land-lord, the ingenious Mr Patrick Miller, found relaxation from the scientific studies and researches in which he so greatly excelled. . . . The poet was accustomed to say that the most happy period of his life was the first winter he spent at Ellisland, for the first time under a roof of his own, with his wife and children about him.'

The poet was proving the truth of his own words :

> To make a happy fire-side clime
> > To weans and wife,   *children*
> That's the true pathos and sublime
> > Of human life.

It is known that he composed also another song in honour of Mrs Burns before she took up her residence at Ellisland : 'O were I on Parnassus hill.'

The song is thought to have been composed while the poet was one day gazing towards the hill of Corsincon at the head of Nithsdale, and beyond which though at some distance, was the quiet vale where lived his Bonie Jean.

O, WERE I ON PARNASSUS HILL

> O WERE I on Parnassus hill,
> Or had o' Helicon my fill,
> That I might catch poetic skill,
> > To sing how dear I love thee!
> But Nith maun be my Muse's well,   *must*
> My muse maun be thy bonie sel':
> On Corsincon I'll glow'r and spell,   *gaze*
> > And write how dear I love thee!

Then come, sweet Muse, inspire my lay!
For a' the lee-lang simmer's day,   *livelong*
I couldna sing, I couldna say,
   How much, how dear, I love thee.
I see thee dancing o'er the green—
Thy waist sae jimp, thy limbs sae clean *neat; elegant*
Thy tempting lips, thy roguish een,—   *eyes*
   By Heaven and earth I love thee!

By night, by day, a-field, at hame,
The thoughts o' thee my breast inflame;
And ay I muse and sing thy name,
   I only live to love thee!
Tho' I were doom'd to wander on,
Beyond the sea, beyond the sun;
Till my last, weary sand was run,—
   Till then—and then I love thee!

The Rev. Hamilton Paul says: 'There is nothing in the whole circle of lyric poetry, ancient or modern, to be named with it. It bids defiance to comparison.'

In the course of their married life Jean's fine 'woodnote wild' proved of very practical help to the poet. As his songs were finished she would sing them over and over again until he was satisfied with the effort. To her he read almost every piece he composed, and said on occasion he had profited much by her counsel.

Throughout the years Jean tended the poet faithfully with care and devotion and was much respected. Burns died in poverty, and his whole concern had been for the future welfare of Jean and the children. His country heard the agonized appeal. Public sympathy was roused by the plight of the widow who became the mother of another child on 25th July, four days after her husband's death. Sufficient funds were soon raised to place her beyond all fear of want. She stayed on in the same dingy little house in Dumfries where her husband had died and refused to leave it, until thirty-eight years later, a day came on 26th March 1834, when she was carried out and laid in the stately Burns mausoleum beside her lover—Scotland's National Poet—Robert Burns.

Bonie Jean's song:

COUNTRIE LASSIE

O, gear will buy me rigs o' land;   *riches; ridges*
  And gear will buy me sheep and kye, *cows*
But the tender heart o' leesome love,   *gladsome*
  The gowd and siller canna buy;   *gold and silver*
We may be poor—Robie and I,
  Light is the burden love lays on;
Content and love bring peace and joy—
  What mair hae queens upon a throne?

Maria Whitefoord

1785, age 26

HER FLOWING LOCKS

HER flowing locks—the raven's wing—
    Adown her neck and bosom hing;
How sweet unto that breast to cling,
    And round that neck entwine her!
Her lips are roses wet wi' dew!
    O what a feast her bonie mou'!
Her cheeks a mair celestial hue,
    A crimson still diviner!

THIS small piece, Cunningham says, was an extemporaneous
effusion—a portrait of a young lady, Miss Whitefoord, whose
beauty attracted the poet when he met her one day on the streets
of Mauchline. It was found among his manuscripts and first
printed by Cromek.

THE BRAES O' BALLOCHMYLE

THE Catrine woods were yellow seen,
    The flowers decay'd on Catrine lea;
Nae lav'rock sang on hillock green,   *no lark*
    But nature sicken'd on the e'e: *eye*
Thro' faded groves Maria sang,
    Hersel' in beauty's bloom the while;
And aye the wild-wood echoes rang—
    Fareweel the braes o' Ballochmyle!

39

Low in your wintry beds, ye flowers,
   Again ye'll flourish fresh and fair;
Ye birdies dumb, in with'ring bowers,
   Again ye'll charm the vocal air;
But here, alas! for me nae mair   *no more*
   Shall birdie charm, or floweret smile,—
Fareweel the bonie banks of Ayr!
   Fareweel! fareweel! sweet Ballochmyle!

Burns in his manuscript note says: 'I composed these verses on the amiable and excellent family of Whitefoord leaving Ballochmyle, when Sir John's misfortunes obliged him to sell his estates.' The Maria of the song was Miss Whitefoord, who afterwards became Mrs Cranston.

Peggy Kennedy

1785, age 26

THE BANKS O' DOON

Ye banks and braes o' bonie Doon,
　How can ye bloom sae fresh and fair!
How can ye chant, ye little birds,
　And I sae weary fu' o' care!

Thou'll break my heart, thou warbling bird,
　That wantons thro' the flowering thorn;
Thou minds me o' departed joys,
　Departed never to return.

Aft hae I rov'd by bonie Doon,
　To see the rose and woodbine twine;
And ilka bird sang o' its luve,　　　　　*every*
　And fondly sae did I o' mine.

Wi' lightsome heart I pu'd a rose,　　　*pulled*
　Fu' sweet upon its thorny tree;
And my fause luver staw my rose,　　　*stole*
　But, ah! he left the thorn wi' me.

PEGGY KENNEDY was the daughter of a Carrick laird, Robert
Kennedy of Daljarrock in the parish of Colmonell and a relative
of the wife of Gavin Hamilton, Burns's friend in Mauchline. The
poet was introduced to her when she was on a visit to the Hamil-
tons in Mauchline in the autumn of 1785. She was then a handsome and refined girl of seventeen and was engaged to Captain
(afterwards Colonel) McDoual, younger of Logan, who

41

although only twenty-five years of age represented the oldest and richest family in Galloway. He was also Member of Parliament for the county.

In admiration of her beauty, Burns composed the song 'Young Peggy', and sent it to her with the following letter:

MADAM,—Permit me to present you with the enclosed song as a small, though grateful tribute, for the honour of your acquaintance. I have, in these verses, attempted some faint sketches of your portrait in the unembellished simple manner of descriptive TRUTH.—Flattery, I leave to your LOVERS, whose exaggerating fancies may make them imagine you still nearer perfection than you really are.

Poets, madam, of all mankind, feel most forcibly the powers of BEAUTY; as, if they are really POETS of nature's making, their feelings must be finer, and their taste more delicate than most of the world. In the cheerful bloom of SPRING, or the pensive mildness of AUTUMN; the grandeur of SUMMER, or the hoary majesty of WINTER, the poet feels a charm unknown to the rest of his species. Even the sight of a fine flower, or the company of a fine woman (by far the finest part of God's works below), have sensations for the poetic heart that the HERD of man are strangers to.—On this last account, madam, I am, as in many other things, indebted to Mr Hamilton's kindness in introducing me to you. Your lovers may view you with a wish, I look on you with pleasure; their hearts, in your presence, may glow with desire, mine rises with admiration.

That the arrows of misfortune, however they should, as incident to humanity, glance a slight wound, may never reach your *heart*—that the snares of villainy may never beset you in the road of life—that INNOCENCE may hand you by the path of HONOUR to the dwelling of PEACE, is the sincere wish of him who has the honour to be, etc.   R. B.

YOUNG PEGGY

YOUNG Peggy blooms our boniest lass,
        Her blush is like the morning,
The rosy dawn, the springing grass,
        With pearly gems adorning:

Her eyes outshine the radiant beams
  That gild the passing shower,
And glitter o'er the crystal streams,
  And cheer each fresh'ning flower.

Her lips more than the cherries bright,
  A richer die has grac'd them;
They charm th' admiring gazer's sight
  And sweetly tempt to taste them:
Her smile is as the ev'ning mild,
  When feather'd pairs are courting,
And little lambkins wanton wild,
  In playful bands disporting.

Were Fortune lovely Peggy's foe,
  Such sweetness would relent her,
As blooming spring unbends the brow
  Of surly, savage winter.
Detraction's eye no aim can gain
  Her winning pow'rs to lessen;
And fretful Envy grins in vain,   *spiteful*
  The poison'd tooth to fasten.

Ye Pow'rs of Honour, Love and Truth,
  From ev'ry ill defend her;
Inspire the highly-favor'd Youth
  The destinies intend her;
Still fan the sweet connubial flame
  Responsive in each bosom;
And bless the dear parental name
  With many a filial blossom.

Unfortunately, the cherished hopes of the poet for Peggy's future happiness were never fulfilled.

Her marriage with McDoual was a secret one. Peggy was too trustful, and apparently there had been no 'civil marriage' at all although Peggy believed that she was married. She gave birth to a daughter and implored her so-called lover to avow the marriage. He refused, declared that he was not the father of her child and went off and married the daughter of a Dumfriesshire laird. An action was raised in Court of 'declarator of marriage' and for damages for seduction, but before the case was finished

Peggy died of a broken heart. Three years later the Consistorial Court of the Church declared her marriage legal according to Scots Law, and made the child legitimate. McDoual, however, managed to get a verdict by the Court of Session reversing this decision, but awarded £3,000 in respect of the deceased Peggy and alimentary provision to her child.

Burns has immortalized Peggy Kennedy and her sorrow in the song 'The Banks o' Doon' with the pathetic ending: 'And my fause luver staw my rose, But ah! he left the thorn wi' me.'

There are three versions of the song, the one at the head of this article written at Ellisland being the most popular.

Another version was sent to Mr Ballantyne with the following note: 'While here I sit, sad and solitary, by the side of a fire in a little country inn, and drying my wet clothes, in pops a poor fellow of a sodger, and tells me he is going to Ayr. By Heaven! say I to myself, with a tide of good spirits which the magic of that sound, auld toun o' Ayr, conjured up, I will send my last song to Mr Ballantyne.' Here it is:

[EARLIER VERSION]

YE flowery banks o' bonie Doon,
    How can ye blume sae fair!
How can ye chant, ye little birds,
    And I sae fu' o' care!

Thou'll break my heart, thou bonie bird,
    That sings upon the bough;
Thou minds me o' the happy days
    When my fause luve was true.

Thou'll break my heart, thou bonie bird,
    That sings beside thy mate;
For sae I sat, and sae I sang,
    And wist na o' my fate.

Aft hae I rov'd by bonie Doon,
    To see the woodbine twine;
And ilka bird sang o' its luve,
    And sae did I o' mine.

Wi' lightsome heart I pu'd a rose,
    Fae aff its thorny tree;
And my fause luver staw the rose,
    But left the thorn wi' me.

And here is yet another version:

YE BANKS AND BRAES

Ye banks and braes o' bonie Doon,
    How can ye bloom sae fresh and fair?
How can ye chaunt, ye little birds,
    And I sae weary, fu' o' care?
Ye'll break my heart, ye warbling birds,
    That warble on the flow'ry thorn,
Ye mind me o' departed joys,
    Departed never to return.

Oft hae I roved by bonie Doon,
    By morning and by evening shine,
To hear the birds sing o' their loves,
    As fondly once I sang o' mine;
Wi' lightsome heart I stretch'd my hand,
    And pu'd a rose-bud from the tree;
But my fause lover stole the rose,
    And left, and left, the thorn wi' me.

Betty Miller

1786, age 27

Eliza

FROM thee, ELIZA, I must go,
  And from my native shore:
The cruel fates between us throw
  A boundless ocean's roar;
But boundless oceans, roaring wide,
  Between my Love and me,
They never, never can divide
  My heart and soul from thee!

Farewell, farewell, ELIZA dear,
  The maid that I adore!
A boding voice is in mine ear,
  We part to meet no more!
But the latest throb that leaves my heart,
  While Death stands victor by,
That throb, ELIZA, is thy part,
  And thine that latest sigh!

THE heroine of this song was the 'Miss Betty is braw', one of
the Mauchline belles whom the poet has celebrated in epigram-
matic verse. She was born and brought up in Ayrshire, was of an
amiable disposition, and appears to have sympathized with the
poet in all his sufferings and thus raised, says Chambers, a kind
of love, chiefly composed of gratitude, in his bosom. The love,

as in several cases with Burns, was purely poetical. Burns wrote the song prior to his intended departure for the West Indies.

Betty was the sister of Miss Helen Miller, the wife of Dr Mackenzie. She ultimately married a Mr William Templeton and died at Alva in 1827, in the seventy-fourth year of her age.

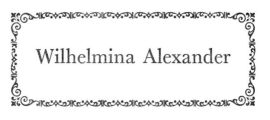

Wilhelmina Alexander

1786, age 27

THE LASS O' BALLOCHMYLE

'Twas even—the dewy fields were green,
  On every blade the pearls hang;
The Zephyr wantoned round the bean,
  And bore its fragrant sweets alang:
In every glen the mavis sang,
  All Nature listening seemed the while;
Except where green-wood echoes rang
  Amang the braes o' Ballochmyle.

With careless step I onward strayed,
  My heart rejoiced in Nature's joy;
When musing in a lonely glade,
  A maiden fair I chanced to spy:
Her look was like the morning's eye,
  Her air like Nature's vernal smile,
Perfection whispered passing by,
  'Behold the lass o' Ballochmyle!'

Fair is the morn in flowery May,
  And sweet is night in Autumn mild;
When roving thro' the garden gay,
  Or wandering in the lonely wild:
But woman, Nature's darling child!
  There all her charms she does compile
Even there her other works are foil'd
  By the bonie lass o' Ballochmyle!

O! had she been a country maid,
   And I the happy country swain;
'Tho' sheltered in the lowest shed
   That ever rose on Scotland's plain,
Thro' weary winter's wind and rain
   With joy, with rapture, I would toil,
And nightly to my bosom strain
   The bonie lass o' Ballochmyle!

Then pride might climb the slippery steep,
   Where fame and honours lofty shine;
And thirst of gold might tempt the deep,
   Or downward seek the Indian mine;
Give me the cot below the pine,
   To tend the flocks, or till the soil,
And every day have joys divine
   With the bonie lass o' Ballochmyle!

WILHELMINA, the sister of Claud Alexander—who purchased the estate of Ballochmyle in 1783—was considerably above the poet's station in life. The circumstances that called forth the song are given in a letter from Burns to Miss Alexander when sending a copy of it to her:

To Miss Alexander.

                      Mossgiel, Nov. 18, 1786.

MADAM,—Poets are such *outré* beings, so much the children of wayward fancy and capricious whim, that I believe the world generally allows them a larger latitude in the laws of propriety than the sober sons of judgment and prudence. I mention this as an apology for the liberties that a nameless stranger has taken with you in the enclosed poem, which he begs leave to present you with. Whether it has poetical merit any way worthy of the theme, I am not the proper judge; but it is the best my abilities can produce; and, what to a good heart will, perhaps, be a superior grace, it is as sincere as fervent.

The scenery was nearly taken from real life, though I daresay, madam, you do not recollect it, as I believe you scarcely noticed the poetic *rêveur* as he wandered by you. I had roved out, as chance directed, in the favourite haunts of my muse, on the banks of the Ayr, to view nature in all the gaiety of the vernal year. The evening sun was flaming over the distant western hills; not a breath stirred the crimson opening blossom or the verdant spreading leaf. It was a golden moment for a poetic heart. I listened to the feathered warblers, pouring their harmony on every hand, with a congenial kindred regard, and frequently turned out of my path, lest I should disturb their little songs, or frighten them to another station. Surely, said I to myself, he must be a wretch indeed who, regardless of your harmonious endeavour to please him, can eye your elusive flights to discover your secret recesses, and to rob you of all the property nature gives you—your dearest comforts, your helpless nestlings. Even the hoary hawthorn twig that shot across the way, what heart at such a time but must have been interested in its welfare, and wished it preserved from the rudely-browsing cattle, or the withering eastern blast? Such was the scene, and such the hour, when in a corner of my prospect I spied one of the fairest pieces of nature's workmanship that ever crowned a poetic landscape or met a poet's eye, those visionary bards excepted who hold converse with aerial beings! Had Calumny and Villainy taken my walk, they had at that moment sworn eternal peace with such an object.

What an hour of inspiration for a poet! It would have raised plain dull historic prose into metaphor and measure.

The enclosed song ('The Bonie Lass of Ballochmyle') was the work of my return home; and perhaps it but poorly answers what might have been expected from such a scene.

R. B.

Much to the mortification of Burns, Miss Alexander took no notice of either the letter, or the song! I do not think, however, that this was due entirely to indifference. It was very likely due to the fact that she did not want her name to be associated with Burns, and also to the influence her brother Claud had upon her. He was no friend of such a humble person as the poor, ploughman poet. Later, in the Grenriddel volume of his letters, Burns copied in one to Miss Alexander with a note also about her brother appended: Speaking of Claud, Wilhelmina's 'great

HIGHLAND MARY
parting with Burns
(*Page 54*)

MINCE COLLOPS CLOSE, GREENOCK
where Highland Mary died
(*Page 54*)

brother' as he calls him, he tells us that he has met him 'on more equal terms of respectability'. He feels he has no grounds to complain of the want of attention to himself. Of such men, he goes on, 'when Fate swore that their purses should be full, Nature was equally positive that their heads should be empty. Men of their fashion', he ironically comments, 'are surely incapable of being impolite!! "Ye canna' mak' a silk purse o' a sow's lug."'

Hard words to be sure, but probably justified. Wilhelmina was about thirty-one years of age at this time. She never married. In her later years she kept the song and letter in a glass case and exhibited them with great pride to her friends.

She died in Glasgow in 1843 at the ripe age of eighty-eight years, and a nephew of hers has erected a rustic grotto and seat at the spot where the poet is regarded has having seen her passing by. The grotto contains a facsimile of the manuscript of two verses of the song.

E

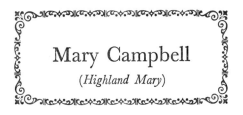

Mary Campbell
(*Highland Mary*)

1786, age 27

AFTON WATER

FLOW gently, sweet Afton, among thy green braes,
Flow gently, I'll sing thee a song in thy praise;
My Mary's asleep by thy murmuring stream,
Flow gently, sweet Afton, disturb not her dream.

Thou stock-dove, whose echo resounds thro' the glen,
Ye wild whistling blackbirds in yon thorny den,
Thou green-crested lapwing thy screaming forbear,
I charge you disturb not my slumbering fair.

How lofty, sweet Afton, thy neighbouring hills,
Far mark'd with the courses of clear, winding rills;
There daily I wander as noon rises high,
My flocks and my Mary's sweet cot in my eye.

How pleasant thy banks and green valleys below,
Where wild in the woodlands the primroses blow;
There oft as mild ev'ning weeps over the lea,
The sweet scented birk shades my Mary and me.   *birch*

Thy crystal stream, Afton, how lovely it glides,
And winds by the cot where my Mary resides;
How wanton thy waters her snowy feet lave,
As gathering sweet flowerets she stems thy clear wave.

Flow gently, sweet Afton, among thy green braes,
Flow gently, sweet river, the theme of my lays;
My Mary's asleep by thy murmuring stream,
Flow gently, sweet Afton, disturb not her dream!

OF THIS sweet song both Gilbert Burns, the poet's eldest brother, and a daughter of Mrs Dunlop affirm that they frequently heard Burns say that it was written upon the dearly loved and long-remembered 'Highland Mary'.

Mary Campbell was born in a thatched cottage, which no longer stands, on the farm of Auchamore in the parish of Dunoon, Argyll, the eldest of eight children born to her parents, who were married in 1762. Her father, Archibald Campbell, was a hand on board a revenue cutter plying on the west coast, in which he lost an eye, and was pensioned off. The family resided at Campbeltown and Ardrossan as well as Dunoon at different times. In her childhood Mary lived for some time at Lochranza, Arran, in the home of the Rev. David Campbell, a relative of her mother.

Mary is then said to have been a dairymaid at Coilsfield, the seat of Col. Hugh Montgomerie, poetically called by Burns 'the Castle o' Montgomerie', and then in 1785 to have entered service as a nursemaid in the household of Gavin Hamilton, Mauchline. Having learned there the finer branches of housework, she finally returned to the Castle as laundry-maid. It was at Tarbolton, however, that she first became acquainted with and learned to love the poet.

'She had no worldly wealth,' says Mr Bannatyne, 'no particular intellectual gifts, but she had those qualities of heart and mind which gained and retained the affections of the poet.'

Her association with Burns commenced at a time of extreme bitterness and disappointment in Burns's life, a time when he saw nothing left to him but to leave his native land. It was then that Mary entered into his life, a sweet, guileless, but extremely loyal and intensely devoted Highland lassie, and she it was who helped to resurrect in him a proper appreciation of the true value of things, and to some extent his faith in mankind and confidence in himself and his destiny. Of her Burns said 'her bosom is fraught with truth, honour, constancy, and love'.

Burns at this time believed that his marriage to Jean Armour had been disannulled, and in the desperateness of his circumstances he had resolved to go to Jamaica, and as Mary was leaving her place of employment they arranged to spend together 'one day of parting love'. On the second Sunday of May 1786, Burns and Mary stood on opposite banks of a tiny stream, the Faile, just where it is about to fall into the River Ayr, and there, beneath the gay green birk and the sweet-scented hawthorn overhanging the stream, they plighted their troth in the ancient Scottish fashion. They laved their hands in the water—an emblem of purity—and clasping them from bank to bank, holding Mary's Bible between them, signifying that as long as that stream continued to run and as long as that book held true, so long would they be true to one another; and, as a further solemn pledge of mutual devotion, they exchanged Bibles ere they bade their 'last farewell'. The Bible presented by Burns to Mary is now in the monument at Alloway. It is in two volumes. On a blank leaf of one is inscribed in Burns's well-known handwriting: 'And ye shall not swear by My Name falsely; I am the Lord.' (Lev. xix. 12.) On the second volume the same hand has written: 'Thou shall not forswear thyself, but shall perform unto the Lord thine oaths.' (Matt. v. 33.) On the blank leaf of both volumes, now almost illegible, is impressed the poet's masonic sign, with his signature 'Robert Burns, Mossgiel'.

This was the last time that Burns and his Highland Mary ever met. She returned to her home at Campbeltown, came back by way of Greenock, nursed a brother who was sick of a malignant fever, herself caught the contagion and died there on 20th October 1786. She was interred in the West Church burial ground, Greenock, where a beautiful monument has been erected to her memory. A magnificent statue of Highland Mary has also been erected on the Castle hill, Dunoon, in which she is depicted as looking over to Ayrshire. All the beauty, tenderness and pathos of Burns are gathered up in his two laments— 'To Mary in Heaven' and 'Highland Mary'.

TO MARY IN HEAVEN

MY MARY, DEAR DEPARTED SHADE

THOU ling'ring star, with less'ning ray,
   That lov'st to greet the early morn,
Again thou usher'st in the day
   My Mary from my soul was torn.
O Mary! dear departed shade!
   Where is thy place of blissful rest?
See'st thou thy lover lowly laid?
   Hear'st thou the groans that rend his breast?

That sacred hour can I forget,
   Can I forget the hallow'd grove,
Where by the winding Ayr we met,
   To live one day of parting love!
Eternity can not efface
   Those records dear of transports past;
Thy image at our last embrace,—
   Ah! little thought we 'twas our last!

Ayr, gurgling, kiss'd his pebbled shore,
   O'erhung with wild woods thick'ning green;
The fragrant birch, and hawthorn hoar
   Twin'd amorous round the raptur'd scene;
The flowers sprang wanton to be prest,
   The birds sang love on every spray;
Till too, too soon, the glowing west
   Proclaim'd the speed of wingèd day.

Still o'er these scenes my mem'ry wakes,
   And fondly broods with miser care!
Time but th' impression stronger makes,
   As streams their channels deeper wear.
My Mary! dear departed shade!
   Where is thy place of blissful rest?
See'st thou thy lover lowly laid?
   Hear'st thou the groans that rend his breast?

John Gibson Lockhart styled this song 'The noblest of all Burns's ballads'. On 20th October 1789, Burns's wife, Bonie Jean, noticed that her husband was beginning to grow sad about something. It was the third anniversary of Mary's death. She saw him go out and wander solitary along the banks of the Nith contemplating the sky that was clear and starry. Then his eye seemed fixed on a beautiful planet that shone with extra-ordinary brilliance. He tarried at that spot during most of the night screening himself on the lee-side of a corn-stack from the cutting edge of the night wind. Immediately on entering the house in the early hours of the morning he sat down at his desk and wrote as they now stand, with all the ease of one copying from memory, the verses of the above sublime and pathetic song.

Mr Archibald Munro, in his book *The Story of Burns and Highland Mary*, tells us that on one occasion the poet's sister, Mrs Begg, who lived near Alloway Bridge, was visited by two strangers who seemed very much interested in Burns's poetry. They inquired for the various editions of his work and the elder of the two asked permission to read aloud a poem which interested him very much. He then read or intoned 'To Mary in Heaven', at the conclusion of which all were in tears. Mrs Begg desired to know the reader's name, when his companion informed her that he desired to travel incognito. But when on departing they reached the door, the reader took the aged lady's hand and said: 'Mrs Begg, I have reasons for withholding my name on certain occasions, and I trust that so far as you are concerned my name may remain a secret here for a few days at least. To the sister of immortal Burns I have now the honour and pleasure of con-fiding my name—Alfred Tennyson.'

Highland Mary

Ye banks, and braes, and streams around
    The castle o' Montgomerie!
Green be your woods, and fair your flowers,
    Your waters never drumlie: *turbid*
There simmer first unfauld her robes,   *unfold*
    And there the langest tarry;
For there I took the last fareweel
    O' my sweet Highland Mary.

How sweetly bloomed the gay green birk,   *birch*
　　How rich the hawthorn's blossom,
As underneath their fragrant shade
　　I clasped her to my bosom!
The golden hours, on angel wings,
　　Flew o'er me and my dearie;
For dear to me, as light and life,
　　Was my sweet Highland Mary.

Wi' mony a vow, and locked embrace,
　　Our parting was fu' tender;
And, pledging aft to meet again,
　　We tore oursel's asunder:
But, oh! fell death's untimely frost,
　　That nipt my flower sae early!
Now green's the sod, and cauld's the clay,
　　That wraps my Highland Mary!

O pale, pale now, those rosy lips,
　　I aft hae kissed sae fondly!
And closed for aye the sparkling glance
　　That dwelt on me sae kindly:
And mouldering now in silent dust
　　That heart that lo'ed me dearly!
But still within my bosom's core
　　Shall live my Highland Mary.

This is another magnificent composition of Burns's passion for his Highland lassie. Writing to Thomson, his publisher, he says: 'The foregoing song "Highland Mary", pleases myself; I think it is in my happiest manner: you will see at first glance that it suits the air. The subject of the song is one of the most interesting passages of my youthful days; and I own that I should be much flattered to see the verses set to an air which would insure celebrity. Perhaps, after all, 'tis the still glowing prejudice of my heart that throws a borrowed lustre over the merits of the composition.' And Thomson in reply says: 'Your verses upon "Highland Mary" are just come to hand; they breathe the genuine spirit of poetry, and, like the music, will last for ever. Such verses, united to such an air, with the delicate harmony of Pleyel superadded, might form a treat worthy of being

presented to Apollo himself. I have heard the sad story of your
Mary: you always seem inspired when you write of her.'

Among other songs that celebrate Highland Mary are the
following:

WILL YE GO TO THE INDIES, MY MARY?

WILL ye go to the Indies, my Mary,
   And leave auld Scotia's shore?
Will ye go to the Indies, my Mary,
   Across th' Atlantic's roar?

O sweet grows the lime and the orange,
   And the apple on the pine;
But a' the charms o' the Indies,
   Can never equal thine.

I hae sworn by the Heavens to my Mary,
   I hae sworn by the Heavens to be true;
And sae may the Heavens forget me,
   When I forget my vow!

O plight me your faith, my Mary,
   And plight me your lily-white hand;
O plight me your faith, my Mary,
   Before I leave Scotia's strand.

We hae plighted our troth, my Mary,
   In mutual affection to join,
And curst be the cause that shall part us!
   The hour and the moment o' time!

'In my early years,' says Burns in a letter to Thomson in 1792,
'when I was thinking of going to the West Indies, I took this
farewell of a dear girl (Highland Mary).'

THE HIGHLAND LASSIE, O

NAE gentle dames, tho' ne'er sae fair,   *no highborn*
Shall ever be my muse's care;
Their titles a' are empty show;
Gie me my Highland Lassie, O.   *give*

CHORUS

Within the glen sae bushy, O,
Aboon the plain sae rashy, O,   *above; full of*
I set me down wi' right gude will,   *good   [rushes*
To sing my Highland Lassie, O.

O were yon hills and valleys mine,
Yon palace and yon gardens fine!
The world then the love should know
I bear my Highland Lassie, O.
    Within the glen, etc.

But fickle fortune frowns on me,
And I maun cross the raging sea;   *must*
But while my crimson currents flow,
I'll love my Highland Lassie, O.
    Within the glen, etc.

Altho' thro' foreign climes I range,
I know her heart will never change,
For her bosom burns with honor's glow,
My faithful Highland Lassie, O.
    Within the glen, etc.

For her I'll dare the billow's roar;
For her I'll trace a distant shore;
That Indian wealth may lustre throw
Around my Highland Lassie, O.
    Within the glen, etc.

She has my heart, she has my hand,
By secret truth and honor's band!
Till the mortal stroke shall lay me low
I'm thine, my Highland Lassie, O.

    Farewell, the glen sae bushy, O!
    Farewell, the plain sae rashy, O
    To other lands I now must go
    To sing my Highland Lassie, O!

'This', says the poet, 'was a composition of mine before I was at all known in the world. My Highland lassie, Mary, was a warm-hearted, charming young creature as ever blessed a man with generous love.'

A tribute by Archibald Munro in the *Scotsman*, 20th October 1891:

'There is probably no name in Scottish literature that has more tenderly touched the hearts of her countrymen than that of Mary Campbell. Though born of an obscure family, brought up in circumstances little fitted to attract general attention and credited with no achievement that invests heroism with permanent or even temporary distinction, this Highland girl is a brilliant star in the galaxy of Fame, and has become the object of unmingled admiration. She died on 20th October 1786. The lustre of Mary's name, like that of other stars and planets, borrows its fascination from a luminary brighter and greater than itself, and the very obscurity of her earlier condition enlarges by contrast the halo that now encircles her name. Moralists have lauded her virtues, critics have lovingly dropped their satiric shafts when commenting on her life and poets have exhausted their resources in their effort to convey their conceptions of her excellence; but all their contributions to the sum of her praise have taken their origin and complexion from the picture which inspired genius has given of her to the world. The interest created by the association of the heroine's career with that of the gifted lover who has procured for her the honour of poetical immortality is not, it is pleasant to know, confined to the country that gave her birth. All over the British Isles and throughout the English-speaking world her worth, unfortunate fate and her premature death have found admirers and sympathizers as cordial and sincere as any that Caledonia has produced.

'Of the particulars of the life of Mary we have but a very meagre account, and curiously enough it happens that in the locality where from first to last she passed most of her days, little is known and still less recorded of her; while the town where she spent but a few days of her existence has by the mere accident of her death there almost monopolized the attention of her biographers. Official documents as well as consistent traditions have assigned to Dunoon the honour of being her birth-place. Mary was born in the year 1768 in Auchamore or, by interpretation, Bigfield, a space of ground forming the south-western and south-eastern parts of Kirn and Dunoon respectively. A complete transformation in the aspect of the district from what it was as I remember fifty years ago has, with other antique buildings, overtaken the plain but interesting but-an'-ben,[1] where Mary drew her first breath. The spirit of modern improvement is answerable for the disappearance of the notable cottage. Mary's father, who in the earlier years of his manhood was a seaman in a Revenue cruiser, bought and commanded a small sloop for the coal trade between Campbeltown, Troon and other small ports on the Firth of Clyde. Finding the residence of his family at Dunoon to be inconvenient for all parties he had them removed to Campbeltown. At the time of his migration Mary, the eldest of his children, was nearly eight years of age; and her unbroken connection with her new home extended over a little more than a similar number of years. Faithful to the instincts of clanships the Campbells took quarters in the immediate neighbourhood of one Elizabeth Campbell or M'Neill, a cousin of the head of the family. It is from Julia M'Neill, a daughter of Elizabeth Campbell, that the later inquirers into the history of Highland Mary, while resident in Campbeltown, have received whatever amount of information existed there regarding her. In my early school days I frequently saw Julia, as well as many others who were personally acquainted with the whole of the family to which Mary Campbell belonged. Mrs M'Neill's house as well as Mrs Campbell's stood in Broombrae at the head of Saddell Street. It is only a few years since the tenement was removed to make way for the present more substantial erection.

'According to Miss M'Neill's statement, which has been corroborated by others who had knowledge of the case, Mary Campbell was a great favourite with every one that knew her—a distinction which she owed to her pleasant manners, sweet temper and obliging disposition. Her figure was graceful; the cast of her face was singularly delicate and of fair complexion, and her eyes which were bluish and lustrous had a remarkably winning expression. The readers of the brief account of her

[1] But-an'-ben: house with outer and inner room.

given by Burns's biographers are aware that sincerity was a feature of the maiden, on which her mother in after years used to dilate with peculiar complacency; and her school companions took special note of her love of peace. Possessed of good natural abilities and faithful to her duties as a pupil she was always able to gain a prominent position in her class; but should a dispute arise at any time as to her right to occupy it, she was prepared to surrender it with right goodwill in the interests of peace and to pacify the probably unreasonable disputant. This spirit of conciliation was such a noticeable trait in her character and was so highly appreciated by her schoolmates and others that, in accordance with the practice of the place, where anyone who is noted for qualities either good or bad is known simply by his Christian name, she came to be recognized by the distinction of "Mary" only. Liberality was also a ruling trait in Mary's character. Of the presents which her father was accustomed to bring home from the various ports he visited, his eldest child was sure to receive the most and best. These partial favours were offered her for her assiduity and devotion to her mother in the discharge of domestic duties. It was not in the girl's power, however, to retain for her own use and pleasure the tokens of another's kindness to herself. Other hands than Mary's were often seen to handle and possess presents not originally intended for them. It thus became a common remark among the knowing ones of the neighbourhood that Mary was too good for this world and could not live long.

'To the unutterable grief of the whole family it was arranged that she was to go to service in a household somewhat distant from home. Her new sphere of duty was in Coilsfield or Montgomerie Castle, in the immediate vicinity of Tarbolton, in the county of Ayr. For this position she was indebted to a Campbeltown lady, the celebrated Miss Arbuckle, who became by marriage a member of the Eglinton family. At the adjacent Parish Church of Tarbolton, Mary used to worship on Sundays with other members of the Coilsfield household, although her acquaintance with the English language was somewhat imperfect; her pronunciation of it, indeed, was so tainted with the Gaelic accent that she soon obtained the more familiar name of Highland Mary. Other celebrities in Burns's diary, such as John

Wilson, the whipper-in, Dr Hornbook, James Humphrey and
John Lees, were numbered among the congregation that met in
the Clachan Church. Burns, who resided in a farm almost
equidistant from the kirks of Mauchline and Tarbolton, seems
to have divided his Sabbaths between these kirks according to
other considerations, as has been hinted, than the reputation
of their preachers or the quality of their sermons. In the latter
church, and shortly after her arrival, the poet saw the interesting young stranger, was charmed with her appearance and
propriety of conduct, and was of course desirous of making her
acquaintance. One of Mary's noticeable habits during the
church service was a close attention to her Bible while the
minister was reading from it or referring to passages illustrative
of his text. It has been conjectured that her loyal observance of
this important duty may have suggested to the mind of the poet
the exchange of Bibles which took place on a subsequent and
memorable occasion.

'There survived till very recently in the neighbourhood of
Montgomerie Castle, an elderly and intelligent gentleman, who
learned from a contemporary of the period the circumstances in
which Burns sought and obtained an introduction to his new
"fancy". In those days a pining swain might have an oppor-
tunity of unburdening his overweighted feelings towards the
object of his regard by the aid of a "blackfoot"—a kind of
official who could in many cases promote a crony's interests and
attend to his own at the same time. In the course of a visit to his
sweetheart, a blackfoot could secure her influence with a female
fellow-servant to consent to a meeting with a companion of his
who was sighing for an interview.

'It was thus that Burns got the coveted introduction—a
favour which his ready wit, his fascinating eyes and impassioned
eloquence improved to the utmost. It so happens that the
individual who in early youth did such yeoman service to Burns
in the capacity of blackfoot exercised in a later age his valuable
talents in favour of the gentleman I have referred to. A series
of extremely diverting incidents connected with the visits
of Burns and of his guide, philosopher and friend to their
respective charmers were among the old gentleman's favourite
reminiscences.

'The intimacy between Burns and Mary ripened, as every record tells, into the tenderest bonds of mutual affection. At a distance of a few yards from the western side of the castle and close to the footpath, there was formerly a thorn tree, whose stem divided into three equally shaped branches and under whose ample shade the lovers were wont to meet. The tree was by turns called "Burns's Thorn" and "Mary's Tryst". The position of the thorn and the attitude of the lovers on a seat beneath its branches are well represented in the *Caledonian Muse*, compiled, edited and published, within a dozen years after the poet's death, by Mr George Thomson, his celebrated correspondent. The view of the thorn, the lovers and the surrounding scenery is exceedingly pleasing. A few years ago the print in Mr Thomson's own copy of the musical compilation, which was his own and Burns's joint production, was cut out of its venerable place and presented to me by his elder daughter, then in the ninety-sixth year of her age. A tree so affectingly associated with the courting days of Burns was sure to tempt the cupidity of the relic-hunter, who in the course of years played havoc with it. . . .

'The Bible presented by Burns on the occasion—described earlier—of his final meeting with Mary, has, after crossing the Atlantic twice and experiencing a singularly eventful career, found its permanent resting-place in the monument on the banks of the Ayr. Fifty years ago, in consequence of the faint association of the lovers' names in the public mind, comparatively little notice was taken of the volumes, or of the precious autograph inscription with which they were assigned to Mary. Since that period, however, there has been, to my certain knowledge, a constantly increasing accession to the tribute of respect paid to her memory. The volumes in the monument are the first and most engrossing objects of attention and curiosity with visitors and the last to re-engage their gaze as they retire. "Time but the impression stronger makes as streams their channels deeper wear." The only source of regret—and it is a keen one—which the visitor experiences on quitting the case where the volumes are exhibited, is the circumstance that Mary's similar gift to Burns is not seen beside them. What has become of that volume, with appropriate texts of Scripture inscribed by Mary's own hand, is a deep mystery and is likely to remain so. Not even that scrap of autograph survives her romantic career. What would not the lovers of romance and poetry give to have access to such a relic! With regard to the extant volumes, it may be observed that a very remarkable change is taking place in the appearance of the poet's handwriting in them. Years ago the characters were clear and distinct, though delicate, as was the characteristic of his penmanship generally at the period when he wrote them; but on recently inspecting them I was surprised and grieved to observe a very decided process of effacement going on. Some of the lighter turns and strokes are so obscure as scarcely to be legible. In the course of a few more years they will at this rate become altogether invisible. Such a consummation would be simply deplorable. The exhibition of the book without the exposure of the autograph should satisfy the public, in consideration of the gain that would be secured. On very important occasions the volumes might be opened for a short time. This course has been adopted in the case of a Burns book in the Mechanics' Library in Dumfries, and with excellent results—the letters seem to be regaining their former clearness.

'At the beginning of the autumn of 1786 Mary went to Campbeltown to make preparations for her contemplated change in life, and there remained till the beginning of October, when she returned to Greenock accompanied by her father. The correspondence that passed between her and her betrothed between August and October must have been of the most interesting character. What it was cannot now be known. The letters received by Mary were religiously preserved by her, and afterwards affectionately treasured by her family. Many years later, however, when the poet's reputation declined and taunts were hurled at the Campbells on account of their connection with him, Mary's elder brother got forcible possession of the priceless collection and, amid the remonstrances and even the execrations of the rest of the household, committed it to the flames. The recent loss by some means or other of the box in which Mary stowed away her lover's letters has occasioned her few surviving relatives much regret, as it was the last relic they possessed.

'Mary's tragic fate shortly after her return to Greenock is

known to everybody. No intelligent and sympathetic emigrant or foreigner on a tour thinks of quitting the old country without paying a visit to her hallowed grave. October 20th is the anniversary of the heroine's death, as well as of the date of its commemoration by our national bard.'

EUPHEMIA MURRAY
(Page 67)

CHLOE
Jean Lorimer
(*Page 113*)

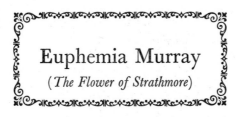

Euphemia Murray
(*The Flower of Strathmore*)

1787, age 28

Blythe was She

CHORUS

Blythe, blythe and merry was she,
   Blythe was she butt and ben;   *by out and by in*
Blythe by the banks of Earn,
   And blythe in Glenturit glen.

By Ochtertyre grows the aik,   *oak*
   On Yarrow banks, the birken shaw;   *birch woods*
But Phemie was a bonier lass,
   Than braes o' Yarrow ever saw.
     Blythe, etc.

Her looks were like a flow'r in May,
   Her smile was like a simmer morn;
She tripped by the banks of Earn,
   As light's a bird upon a thorn.
     Blythe, etc.

Her bonie face it was as meek
   As ony lamb upon a lea;
The evening sun was ne'er sae sweet
   As was the blink o' Phemie's e'e.   *glance*
     Blythe, etc.

The Highland hills I've wander'd wide,
And o'er the Lawlands I hae been;
But Phemie was the blythest lass
That ever trode the dewy green.
Blythe, etc.

PHEMIE was born at Lintrose, the only daughter of Mungo Murray. In 1794 she married the Hon. David Smythe, a judge of the Court of Session. She was popularly known in the community by the appellation 'The Flower of Strathmore' and Burns first met her on a visit he paid to the house of her uncle, Sir William Murray, of Ochtertyre. She was a charming young lady, eighteen years of age at that time, and the poet seems to have been fascinated by her beauty and affability. In her praise, during his Highland tour of 1787, he composed the above delightful song, 'Blythe, Blythe, and Merry was She'.

In his work *Perthshire in Bygone Days*, Mr P. R. Drummond says: 'I confess having tried covertly to conjure up visions of the poet and the lady strolling about the braes of Ochtertyre— she listening to conversation that never failed to fascinate, and he basking in rays to which his heart ever turned with as much certainty as the needle turns to the Pole. The lady's amiable and kind-hearted sister told me some charming reminiscences of Burns—how she met him at Sir James Hunter Blair's, when she was young, and perhaps rather handsome, and how she blushed and shrank from the gaze that followed her on being placed next to the poet, and of his manly and easy bearing, and how his eyes glowed like live coals when his own songs were sung.'

A pure, bright, vivacious young queen was Phemie.

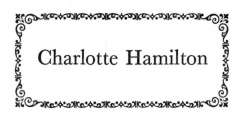

Charlotte Hamilton

1787, age 28

THE BANKS OF THE DEVON

How pleasant the banks of the clear-winding Devon,
  With green-spreading bushes and flow'rs blooming fair!
But the boniest flow'r on the banks of the Devon
  Was once a sweet bud on the braes of the Ayr.

Mild be the sun on this sweet-blushing Flower,
  In the gay, rosy morn as it bathes in the dew;
And gentle the fall of the soft vernal shower,
  That steals on the evening each leaf to renew!

O spare the dear blossom, ye orient breezes,
  With chill, hoary wing as ye usher the dawn!
And far be thou distant, thou reptile that seizes
  The verdure and pride of the garden or lawn!

Let Bourbon exult in his gay, gilded Lilies,
  And England triumphant display her proud Rose;
A fairer than either adorns the green valleys
  Where Devon, sweet Devon, meandering flows.

'THESE verses', says Burns in his notes in the *Musical Museum*,
'were composed on a charming girl, Miss Charlotte Hamilton,
who is now married to James M. Adair, physician. She is sister
to my worthy friend, Gavin Hamilton of Mauchline, and was
born on the banks of the Ayr, but was, at the time I wrote these
lines, residing at Harvieston, in Clackmannanshire, on the
romantic banks of the little river Devon.' Dr Adair, who was a
relative of Mrs Dunlop, describes his introduction to Charlotte

thus: 'The ladies at Harvieston had a great washing-day when
I and the poet arrived, but they contrived, notwithstanding, to
do the honours of hospitality with grace. The result was my
marriage in 1789.'

Writing to Miss Peggy Chalmers, Charlotte's cousin, Burns
says: 'I am determined to pay Charlotte a poetic compliment, if
I could hit on some glorious old Scottish air. I intend to make it
descriptive of some kind; the whining cant of love, except in real
passion, and by a masterly hand, is to me as insufferable as the
preaching cant of old Father Smeaton, Whig-minister of
Kilmaurs. Darts, flames, cupids, loves, graces, and all that
farango are just a Mauchline sacrament—a senseless rabble.' A
month later he writes, intimating that the poetic compliment is
now completed: 'I won't say the poetry is first-rate, though I
am convinced it is very well; and, what is not always the case
with compliments to ladies, it is not only sincere but just.' The
song is that entitled 'The Banks of the Devon'. Again, 'Of
Charlotte', he writes to her half-brother, 'I cannot speak in
common terms of admiration. She is not only beautiful but
lovely. Her form is elegant; her features not regular, but they
have the smile of sweetness and the settled complacency of good
nature in the highest degree; and her complexion, now that she
has happily recovered her wonted health, is equal to Miss
Burnet's. Her eyes are fascinating; at once expressive of good
sense, tenderness, and a noble mind.'

And at another time he says: 'In my conscience, I believe
that my heart has been so oft on fire that it is absolutely vitrified.
I look on the sex with something like the admiration with which
I regard the starry sky in a frosty December night. As for friendship, you and Charlotte have given me pleasure—permanent
pleasure—which the world cannot give nor take away, I hope,
and which will outlast the heavens and the earth.'

FAIREST MAID ON DEVON BANKS

CHORUS

Fairest maid on Devon banks,
Crystal Devon, winding Devon,
Wilt thou lay that frown aside,
And smile as thou wert wont to do?

FULL well thou knowest I love thee dear,
Couldst thou to malice lend an ear?
O did not love exclaim, 'Forbear,
 Nor use a faithful lover so'?
  Fairest maid, etc.

Then come, thou fairest of the fair,
Those wonted smiles, O let me share;
And by thy beauteous self I swear,
 No love but thine my heart shall know.
  Fairest maid, etc.

In this song—composed during the last few days of his life when prostrate with illness and oppressed with poverty—his mind wandered to the banks of the Devon, where he had spent some happy days, when in the full flush of fame, in the company of the lovely Charlotte Hamilton. He had been unfit for his duties as an Excise Officer for some time and was on half-pay. He was in debt to a haberdasher for his volunteer uniform, and for some clothes for his children. The haberdasher, hearing of his serious illness, which was likely to be fatal, instituted at once a lawsuit against him.

The song proved to be his last. It was written on 12th July 1796. He had been to Brow on the Solway Firth to see if sea-bathing would help him, but this proved in no way beneficial. He was in such a poor state of health that he could hardly hold his pen, as is evidenced by the handwriting of the song and the letter he sent with it to Thomson, his publisher in Edinburgh, imploring him for God's sake to lend him £5 to prevent the haberdasher from putting him in jail. Nine days after, 21st July 1796, he died, aged thirty-seven and a half years.

Charlotte died, prematurely, in 1806.

Miss Ferrier

1787, age 28

NAE HEATHEN NAME

NAE heathen name shall I prefix
    Frae Pindas or Parnassus;
Auld Reekie dings them a' to sticks,   *Edinburgh; knocks*
    For rhyme-inspiring lasses.

Jove's tunefu' dochters three times three, *daughters*
    Made Homer deep their debtor;
But, gi'en the body half an e'e,   *given; eye*
    Nine Ferriers wad done better!   *would have*

Last day my mind was in a bog,
    Down George's Street I stoited;   *tottered*
A creeping cauld prosaic fog
    My very senses doited.   *muddled*

Do what I dought to set her free,   *could*
    My saul lay in the mire;   *soul*
Ye turned a neuk—I saw your e'e—   *corner, nook . . . eye*
    She took the wing like fire!

The mournfu' sang I here enclose,
    In gratitude I send you;
And pray in rhyme as weel as prose,—
    May a' that's gude attend you!   *good*

THIS song was sent to Miss Ferrier enclosing an Elegy composed by Burns on Sir J. H. Blair.

During the poet's sojourn in Edinburgh his Muse of fire appears never to have ascended its highest heaven of invention. A few days after the death of his patron, Sir James Hunter Blair, he was wandering in a musing mood along George Street, which was at that time so remote from the great centre of business as to be considered almost in the country, when he accidentally met Miss Ferrier, eldest daughter of Mr John Ferrier, W.S., one of his warmest patrons. In the sparkling eyes of this young lady, who afterwards married General Samuel Graham, the poet seems to have found the inspiration he was in search of.

Clarinda

(*Mrs Agnes McLehose*)

1787–1794

AE FOND KISS

AE fond kiss, and then we sever,—   *one*
Ae fareweel, and then—for ever!
Deep in heart-wrung tears I'll pledge thee!
Warring sighs and groans I'll wage thee!

Who shall say that fortune grieves him,
While the star of hope she leaves him?
Me, nae cheerfu' twinkle lights me,—   *no*
Dark despair around benights me.

I'll ne'er blame my partial fancy,
Naething could resist my Nancy;
But to see her was to love her—
Love but her, and love for ever.

Had we never lov'd sae kindly—
Had we never lov'd sae blindly—
Never met—or never parted,
We had ne'er been broken-hearted!

Fare-thee-weel, thou first and fairest!
Fare-thee-weel, thou best and dearest!
Thine be ilka joy and treasure,   *every*
Peace, Enjoyment, Love, and Pleasure!

74

Ae fond kiss, and then we sever!
Ae fareweel, alas! for ever!
Deep in heart-wrung tears I'll pledge thee!
Warring sighs and groans I'll wage thee!

THE 'Clarinda' episode is an important period in the life of Burns. She seems to have regarded the poet as a disengaged man, and no doubt Burns himself considered at this time that he was freed from his union with Jean Armour. Clarinda on the other hand considered that the removal of her besotted and licentious husband, Mr McLehose, who had deserted her and gone to the West Indies, meant that she was free, and in all probability she looked forward to a union with the poet. Burns writes of her in the following terms: 'Almighty love still reigns and revels in my bosom, and I am at this moment ready to hang myself for a young Edinburgh widow [Mrs McLehose was not in reality a widow], who has wit and wisdom more murderously fascinating than the stiletto of the Sicilian bandit, or the poisoned arrow of the savage African.'

The words of the late Mr John S. Clarke are worth repeating:
'"Our sweetest songs are those that tell of saddest thought."
——Shelley.

'If this is true, Scotland's sweetest song is "Ae Fond Kiss" by Robert Burns. Its burden is the exquisite pain of hopeless love. Burns wrote it as a final farewell to a Glasgow lassie called Agnes Craig, daughter of a Glasgow surgeon, Dr Andrew Craig, whose ministerial brother became the father of Lord Craig. Nancy's mother was the child of the Rev. John McLaurin of the Ramshorn Kirk, and Agnes received an education in a boarding-school in Edinburgh "befitting one in her station of life". She was born in April 1759, rather more than three months later than the poet. In 1776 she married a Glasgow law agent named McLehose, who, after the birth of three children, deserted her, went to Jamaica, and raised another family of mulatoes.

'In 1787 she was introduced to Robert Burns in Edinburgh and a platonic friendship followed which quickly ripened into love. A remarkable correspondence between them followed, the young lady signing her name Clarinda and the poet signing his Sylvander. The romance ended in 1788 when the poet leased

Ellisland. Passing through Glasgow he wrote to Clarinda from the Black Bull, Argyle-street (corner of Virginia-street) in February.

'In March he was back in Glasgow. In June he took possession of Ellisland, preparing the steading for the reception of Jean Armour, his wife, who had remained in Mauchline. It was in 1791 that he "backward cast his e'e on prospects drear" and wrote the exquisite song, "Ae Fond Kiss", which, wrote Sir Walter Scott, "contains the essence of a thousand love tales".'

To this Mrs Anna Jameson added: 'They are not only worth a thousand romances, but they are in themselves a complete romance; they are the alpha and omega of feeling, and contain the essence of an existence of pain and pleasure distilled into one burning drop.' It is indeed one of the most vehement and impressive outbursts of intense feeling ever written, greatly admired by Arnold and Carlyle. The words have been set to a beautiful and pathetic air and can be sung as a duet as well as a solo.

Burns celebrated Clarinda in a number of songs. Here are a few of the best known:

My Lovely Nancy

Thine am I, my faithful fair,
    Thine, my lovely Nancy;
Every pulse along my veins,
    Every roving fancy.

To thy bosom lay my heart,
    There to throb and languish:
Though despair had wrung its core,
    That would heal its anguish.

Take away these rosy lips,
    Rich with balmy treasure:
Turn away thine eyes of love,
    Lest I die with pleasure.

What is life when wanting love?
  Night without a morning:
Love's the cloudless summer sun,
  Nature gay adorning.

CLARINDA, MISTRESS OF MY SOUL

CLARINDA, mistress of my soul,
  The measur'd time is run!
The wretch beneath the dreary pole
  So marks his latest sun.

To what dark cave of frozen night
  Shall poor Sylvander hie;
Depriv'd of thee, his life and light,
  The sun of all his joy?

We part—but by these precious drops,
  That fill thy lovely eyes!
No other light shall guide my steps
  Till thy bright beams arise.

She, the fair sun of all her sex,
  Has blest my glorious day:
And shall a glimmering planet fix
  My worship to its ray?

Some months after Clarinda had left Edinburgh for the West
Indies to make a last, and what proved to be an unsuccessful
attempt, to live with her profligate husband, when time had
mellowed the poet's passion and absence calmed the tumult of
his feelings, he wrote the following touching pastoral:

MY NANNIE'S AWA'

Now in her green mantle blythe Nature arrays,
And listens the lambkins that bleat o'er the braes,
While birds warble welcome in ilka green shaw;   *every . . . wood*
But to me it's delightless—my Nannie's awa'.

The snawdrap and primrose our woodlands adorn,
And violets bathe in the weet o' the morn: *wet with dew*
They pain my sad bosom, sae sweetly they blaw,   *so*
They mind me o' Nannie—and Nannie's awa'.

Thou laverock that springs frae the dews o' the lawn, *lark*
The shepherd to warn o' the gray-breaking dawn,
And thou mellow mavis that hails the night fa',
Give over for pity—my Nannie's awa'.

Come autumn, sae pensive, in yellow and gray,
And soothe me wi' tidings o' Nature's decay:
The dark dreary winter and wild driving snaw
Alane can delight me—now Nannie's awa'!

Mrs McLehose lived until 1841, her eighty-third year, thus surviving Burns for forty-five years. Until the end of her life she fondly cherished the memory of the poet, 'that great genius' as she calls him in her diary, 25th January 1813, and in another entry, 6th December 1831, she wrote: 'This day I can never forget. Parted with Burns in 1791, never more to meet in this world. May we meet in heaven!'

From the voluminous and unique correspondence between Burns and Clarinda, I have chosen one because it reveals the true religion of Robert Burns:

'I am delighted, charming Clarinda, with your honest enthusiasm for religion. Those of either sex, but particularly the female, who are lukewarm in that most important of all things, "O my soul, come not thou into their secrets!" I feel myself deeply interested in your good opinion, and will lay before you the outlines of my belief. He who is our Author and Preserver, and will one day be our Judge, must be (not for His sake in the way of duty, but from the native impulse of our hearts) the object of our reverential awe and grateful adoration: He is Almighty and all-bounteous, we are weak and dependent; hence prayer and every other sort of devotion.—"He is not willing that any should perish, but that all should come to everlasting life"; consequently it must be in every one's power to embrace His offer of "everlasting life"; otherwise He could not, in justice, condemn those who did not. A mind pervaded, actuated, and governed by purity, truth, and charity, though it does not *merit* heaven, yet is an absolutely necessary prerequisite, without which heaven can neither be obtained nor enjoyed; and, by divine promise, such a mind shall never fail of attaining "everlasting life"; hence the impure, the deceiving, and the uncharitable, extrude themselves from eternal bliss, by their unfitness for enjoying it. The Supreme Being has put the immediate administration of all this, for wise and good ends known to Himself, into the hands of Jesus Christ—a great personage, whose relation to Him we cannot comprehend, but whose relation to us is a guide and Saviour; and who, except for our own obstinacy and misconduct, will bring us all, through various ways, and by various means, to bliss at last.

'These are my tenets, my lovely friend; and which, I think, cannot be well disputed. My creed is pretty nearly expressed in the last clause of Jamie Dean's grace, an honest weaver in Ayrshire: "Lord, grant that we may lead a gude life! for a gude life mak's a gude end; at least it helps weel!" Good night, my dearest Clarinda!'

'SYLVANDER.'

In her old age Clarinda delighted to show to her friends the songs and letters of her loving friend, Robert Burns.

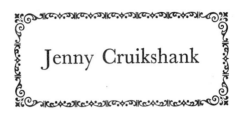

Jenny Cruikshank

1787, age 28

A Rose-bud by my Early Walk

A ROSE-BUD by my early walk,
Adown a corn-inclosed bawk,   *field-path*
Sae gently bent its thorny stalk,
   All on a dewy morning.

Ere twice the shades o' dawn are fled,
In a' its crimson glory spread,
And drooping rich the dewy head,
   It scents the early morning.

Within the bush, her covert nest,
A little linnet fondly prest,
The dew sat chilly on her breast,
   Sae early in the morning.

She soon shall see her tender brood,
The pride, the pleasure o' the wood,
Amang the fresh green leaves bedew'd,
   Awauk the early morning.   *awake*

So thou, dear bird, young Jenny fair!
On trembling string or vocal air,
Shalt sweetly pay the tender care
   That tents thy early morning.   *guards*

So thou, sweet rose-bud, young and gay,
Shalt beauteous blaze upon the day,
And bless the parent's evening ray
    That watch'd thy early morning.

ON 20th October 1787 Burns resided at 30 St James's Square,
Edinburgh, with Mr William Cruikshank, who was one of the
masters of the High School, Edinburgh. Of this visit, Professor
Walker says: 'About the end of October I called for him at the
house of a friend, whose daughter, though not more than twelve,
was a considerable proficient in music. I found him seated by
the harpsichord of this young lady, listening with the keenest
interest to his own verses, which she sang and accompanied,
adjusting them to the music by repeated trials of the effect. In
this occupation he was so totally absorbed that it was difficult
to draw his attention from it for a moment.'

It was in her honour that the poet composed the above song
'A Rosebud by my Early Walk', and also 'Beauteous Rosebud',
which he presented to Jenny along with a book on the blank
page of which he wrote: 'To Miss Cruikshank, a very young
lady.'

Beauteous Rosebud, young and gay,
Blooming in thy early May.

In 1804 she became the wife of Mr James Henderson, a
solicitor in Jedburgh. She died in 1835.

'The air of the song', says Burns, 'is by David Sillar, quon-
dam merchant and now schoolmaster in Irvine.'

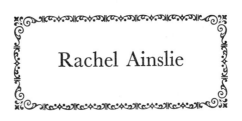

Rachel Ainslie

1787, age 28

MISS RACHEL AINSLIE was the daughter of Mr Robert Ainslie, W.S., whom Burns met during his first visit to Edinburgh and who became one of his warmest friends. In his journal on his tour of the border country on 23rd May 1787, Burns says: 'Found Miss Ainslie, the amiable, the sensible, the good-humoured, the sweet Miss Ainslie, all alone at Berryhill. Heavenly powers, who know the weakness of human hearts, support mine! What happiness must I see only to remind me that I cannot enjoy it! . . . I walk into Duns before dinner, and out to Berryhill in the evening with Miss Ainslie—how well-bred, how frank, how good she is! Charming Rachel! May thy bosom never be wrung by the evils of this life of sorrows, or by the villainy of this world's sins!'

In another place he describes her as 'a little embonpoint, but handsome; her face, particularly her eyes, full of sweetness and good humour'. To this description, he adds: 'She unites three qualities rarely to be found together: keen, solid penetration; sly, witty observation and remark; and the gentlest, most unaffected female modesty.'

On Sunday Burns accompanied the family to church, where he listened to a sermon by 'a minister of strong lungs and pretty judicious remark, but ill-skilled in propriety and altogether unconscious of his want of it, Dr Bowmaker'. Miss Ainslie started to turn over the leaves of her Bible in search of the text he had given out, a text common enough in Burns's day, that contained a severe denunciation of obstinate sinners, when Burns took from his pocket a slip of paper and, having written

on it with his pencil, passed it along the pew to her. Glancing at
it she read:

> Fair maid, you need not take the hint,
>   Nor idle texts pursue;
> 'Twas guilty sinners that he meant,
>   Not angels, such as you!

Miss Ainslie never married but delighted on occasion to show
the epigram to her friends. She died when upwards of sixty
years of age.

G

Margaret Chalmers

1787, age 28

PEGGY

My Peggy's face, my Peggy's form,
The frost of hermit age might warm;
My Peggy's worth, my Peggy's mind,
Might charm the first of human kind:
I love my Peggy's angel air,
Her face so truly, heavenly fair,
Her native grace so void of art;
But I adore my Peggy's heart.

The lily's hue, the rose's dye,
The kindling lustre of an eye;
Who but owns their magic sway?
Who but knows they all decay?
The tender thrill, the pitying tear,
The generous purpose, nobly dear,
The gentle look that rage disarms—
These are all immortal charms.

MY PEGGY'S CHARMS

Where, braving angry winter's storms,
    The lofty Ochils rise;
Far in their shade, my Peggy's charms
    First blest my wondering eyes,—
As one, who, by some savage stream,
    A lonely gem surveys,
Astonish'd, doubly marks it beam,
    With art's most polish'd blaze.

> Blest be the wild, sequester'd shade,
>   And blest the day and hour,
> Where Peggy's charms I first survey'd,
>   When first I felt their pow'r!
> The tyrant death, with grim control,
>   May seize my fleeting breath;
> But tearing Peggy from my soul
>   Must be a stronger death.

THESE two songs were written in praise of Miss Margaret Chalmers, a relative of the poet's friend, Mr Gavin Hamilton of Mauchline. Burns first became acquainted with her at the house of Dr Blacklock, and being of a quiet, amiable disposition and possessed of that 'excellent thing in woman', a delightfully low soft voice, she appears to have left an abiding impression on the heart of the susceptible poet, who called her 'one of the most accomplished of women', and frequently spoke of her with more than common warmth. A relative, describing Peggy to Dr Robert Chalmers, said that 'in early life, when her hazel eyes were large and bright and her teeth white and regular, her face possessed a charm not always the result of the accompaniment of fine features. She was short, but her figure was faultless. Her conversation was cheerful, but intelligent. She talked rarely of books yet greatly liked reading. She spoke readily and well, but preferred listening to others.'

She exercised a refining influence upon the poet and corresponded frequently with him, exchanging confidences.

Peggy would have made an ideal life-partner to the poet. Indeed, when corresponding with Clarinda, Burns wrote on 10th January 1788: 'The name I register in my heart's core is Peggy Chalmers,' and three weeks later Clarinda asked him: 'Why did not such a woman secure your heart?'

Thomas Campbell, the poet, has stated that he was well acquainted with Peggy during her widowhood in after years in Edinburgh and that she confided in him the secret that Burns had once made to her a serious proposal of marriage, but at the time she had been engaged to another, Mr Lewis Hay, an Edinburgh banker, whom she ultimately married on 9th December 1788.

Peggy died a widow at Pau in France in 1843.

Maria Riddel

1788, age 29

THE DAY RETURNS, MY BOSOM BURNS

THE day returns, my bosom burns,
    The blissful day we twa did meet;
Tho' winter wild in tempest toil'd,
    Ne'er summer-sun was half sae sweet.
Than a' the pride that loads the tide,
    And crosses o'er the sultry line;
Than kingly robes, than crowns and globes,
    Heav'n gave me more—it made thee mine!

While day and night can bring delight,
    Or nature aught of pleasure give;
While joys above, my mind can move,
    For thee, and thee alone I live!
When that grim foe of life below,
    Comes in between to make us part;
The iron hand that breaks our band,
    It breaks my bliss—it breaks my heart!

IN a letter to Miss Chalmers from Ellisland, 16th September 1788, Burns enclosed this lyric with the remark 'these two stanzas I made to an air that a musical gentleman of my acquaintance (Captain Riddel of Glenriddel) composed for the anniversary of his wedding-day—7th of November'.

Maria was the daughter of William Woodley, governor and commander-in-chief of St Kitts and the Leeward Isles. She had formed the acquaintance of Walter Riddel, and ultimately became his wife in the West Indies, where he possessed an estate. In 1771 she came to Woodley Park, a mansion house about four miles south of Dumfries, and it was during his Dumfries days that Burns became acquainted with her. She was a talented lady of refinement and culture, interested in literature and a writer of no mean order. Having read Burns's poems she was greatly attracted to him by reason of his genius, with the result that he became a frequent visitor at the mansion house.

Being desirous of publishing a work of her own entitled *Voyages to the Madeira and Leeward Caribee Islands* with sketches of their history, in January 1792 she obtained a letter of introduction from Burns to William Smellie, printer, in Edinburgh. In that letter the poet hits off some of her characteristics. 'She has one unlucky failing,' he says, 'a failing which you will easily observe, as she seems rather pleased with indulging it—and a failing that you will easily pardon, as it is a sin which very much besets yourself—where she dislikes or despairs, she is apt to make no more a secret of it, than where she esteems and respects.'

A quarrel over some trifling incident, however, put an end to the friendship for nearly two years. Scott Douglas has suggested that in his song 'Here's to thy health, my bonie lass', Burns may have been 'mustering all the mysteries of his art with a view to cast his glamour over, and render secure, the affection of Maria Riddel, whom previously he had lampooned so severely'. He pictures her a charming maiden sought after by many suitors.

Here's to thy Health, my Bonie Lass

Here's to thy health, my bonie lass,	
Gude-night and joy be wi' thee!	*good night*
I'll come nae mair to thy bower-door,	*no more*
To tell thee that I lo'e thee:	
O dinna think, my pretty pink,	*do not*
But I can live without thee:	
I vow and swear, I dinna care	
How lang ye look about ye!	*long*

Thou'rt ay sae free informing me
   Thou hast nae mind to marry;
I'll be as free informing thee
   Nae time hae I to tarry:
I ken thy friends try ilka means   *know; every*
   Frae wedlock to delay thee,
Depending on some higher chance—
   But fortune may betray thee!

I ken they scorn my low estate,   *know*
   But that does never grieve me;
For I'm as free as any he,
   Sma' siller will relieve me.   *silver*
I'll count my health my greatest wealth,
   Sae lang as I enjoy it: *so long*
I'll fear nae scant, I'll bode nae want,   *presage*
   Sae lang's I get employment!   *as long as*

But far off fowls hae feathers fair,   *have*
   And ay until ye try them;
Tho' they seem fair, still have a care,
   They may prove waur than I am!   *worse*
But at twal' at night, when the moon shines bright, *twelve*
   My dear, I'll come and see thee;
For the man that loves his mistress weel,   *well*
   Nae travel makes him weary!

That he thought a good deal of Maria's friendship is apparent from such a letter as:

DEAR MADAM,—I meant to have called on you yesternight, but as I edged up to your box-door, the first object which greeted my view was one of those lobster-coated puppies, sitting like another dragon, guarding the Hesperian fruit. On the conditions and capitulations you so obligingly offer, I shall certainly make my weather-beaten rustic phiz a part of your box-furniture on Tuesday; when we may arrange the business of the visit.

Among the profusion of idle compliments, which insidious craft, or unmeaning folly, incessantly offer at your shrine—a shrine, how far exalted above such adoration—permit me, were it but for rarity's sake, to pay you the honest tribute of a warm heart and an independent mind; and to assure you, that I am, thou most amiable, and most accomplished of thy sex, with the most respectful esteem, and fervent regard, thine, etc.

R. B.

For some time after her husband's death, Mrs Riddel resided with friends, particularly the Scotts of Tinwald, but finally went to London, where she married a Mr Fletcher from Ireland. She died in 1820. Before leaving Scotland, however, she had her last interview with the poet. In July 1796 she had gone as a convalescent to Brow for sea-bathing and learned that Burns was also there for the same purpose in the hope that his health might be restored. Immediately she sent an invitation to him to dine with her at her residence and sent her carriage to bring him. It was on this occasion, on entering the room with the stamp of death imprinted on his features, that he asked her: 'Well, madam, have you any commands for the other world?' At this interview both of them became reconciled. Her subsequent eulogy on Burns after his death shows with what admiration she regarded him and his poetic productions.

Elizabeth Burnet

1788, age 29–30

AMONG the eminent literary and philosophical personages who befriended Burns during his visit to Edinburgh was Mr James Burnet, a judge of the Supreme Civil Court of Scotland, under the designation of Lord Monboddo. He was rather eccentric, and had the habit of giving elaborate dinners at his house, to some of which he invited Burns. Here the poet met the beautiful Miss Burnet. On being asked by his friend Mr Geddes: 'Did you admire the young lady?' he replied: 'I admired God Almighty more than ever; Miss Burnet is the most heavenly of all His works.' And writing to his friend, William Chalmers, he says: 'I enclose you two poems, which I have carded and spun since I passed Glenbuck. "Fair Burnet" is the heavenly Miss Burnet, daughter of Lord Monboddo, at whose house I have had the honour to be more than once. There has not been anything nearly like her in all the combinations of beauty, grace, and goodness the great Creator has formed, since Milton's Eve on the first day of her existence!'

One of the poems referred to is his 'Address to Edinburgh', in which the stanza occurs:

> Thy daughters bright thy walks adorn,
>   Gay as the gilded summer sky,
> Sweet as the dewy, milk-white thorn,
>   Dear as the raptured thrill of joy!
> Fair Burnet strikes th' adoring eye,
>   Heaven's beauties on my fancy shine;
> I see the Sire of Love on high,
>   And own His work indeed divine!

She was regarded by everyone in Edinburgh as one of the most beautiful women of her time, and died on 17th June 1790, in the twenty-third year of her age. Later Burns wrote an Elegy on her. Here are two of the verses:

> Life ne'er exulted in so rich a prize
> As Burnet, lovely from her native skies;
> Nor envious death so triumph'd in a blow,
> As that which laid th' accomplished Burnet low.
>
> Thy form and mind, sweet maid, can I forget?
> In richest ore the brightest jewel set!
> In thee, high Heaven above was truest shown,
> And by His noblest work the Godhead best is known.

Ann Masterton

1788, age 29

Beware o' Bonie Ann

Ye gallants bright I rede ye right,   *counsel*
    Beware o' bonie Ann;
Her comely face sae fu' o' grace,   *so full*
    Your hearts she will trepan.   *ensnare*

Her een sae bright, like stars by night,   *eyes*
    Her skin is like the swan;
Sae jimply lac'd her genty waist,   *so tightly; slender*
    That sweetly ye might span.

Youth, grace and love attendant move,
    And pleasure leads the van;
In a' their charms and conquering arms,
    They wait on bonie Ann.

The captive bands may chain the hands,
    But Love enslaves the man;
Ye gallants braw, I rede you a',   *fine*
    Beware o' bonie Ann.

'I composed this song', says Burns, 'out of compliment to Miss Ann Masterton, the daughter of my friend, Mr Allan Masterton of the High School, Edinburgh, and composer of the air "Strathallan's Lament".'

Ann married a medical man, Dr Derbishire, who resided first in Bath and subsequently in London.

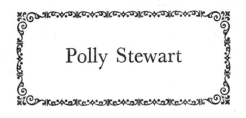

Polly Stewart

1788, age 29

LOVELY POLLY STEWART

CHORUS

O lovely Polly Stewart,
O charming Polly Stewart,
There's ne'er a flower that blooms in May
That's half so fair as thou art.

THE flower it blaws, it fades, it fa's,   *blows; falls*
   And art can ne'er renew it;
But worth, and truth, eternal youth
   Will gie to Polly Stewart.   *give*
     O lovely, etc.

May he, whase arms shall fauld thy charms, *enfold*
   Possess a leal and true heart!   *loyal*
To him be given to ken the Heaven,   *know*
   He grasps in Polly Stewart!
     O lovely, etc.

THE 'Lovely Polly Stewart' of this song was the daughter of
Mr William Stewart, the factor of Closeburn estates, and a
neighbour of the poet's at Ellisland farm. She was only sixteen
years of age when Burns first met her. While still in her teens
she married a young man who was totally unworthy of her
affection. Some scrape he had got into compelled him to
abscond, and he died abroad. Polly next contracted a quasi-
matrimonial alliance with a young man, George Welsh, but

93

the two did not get on well together. She was of a gay, pleasure-loving temperament, whereas he was a sober, stern believer in the seriousness of life. Quarrels ensued, and the upshot was that they separated in 1806, and Polly went to reside with her father, who had settled in Maxwelltown. There she fell in love with a prisoner of war, a handsome Swiss officer named Fleitz, with whom she went abroad. Burns's wish for her was never fulfilled. After many wanderings she died in Florence in 1847.

The chorus of the song was written by Burns with his dia-mond-pointed pen on a window pane of the upper parlour in the Globe Inn, Dumfries.

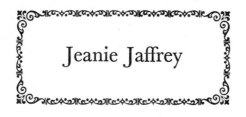

Jeanie Jaffrey

1789, age 30

The Blue-e'ed Lassie

I GAED a waefu' gate yestreen,[1]
  A gate, I fear, I'll dearly rue;
I gat my death frae twa sweet een,   *eyes*
  Twa lovely een o' bonie blue.   *two*
'Twas not her golden ringlets bright—
  Her lips, like roses wat wi' dew—   *wet*
Her heaving bosom, lily-white,—
  It was her een sae bonie blue!   *eyes so*

She talk'd, she smil'd, my heart she wil'd, *beguiled*
  She charm'd my soul—I wist na how;
And ay the stound, the deadly wound,   *pang*
  Cam frae her een sae bonie blue,   *came from*
But, spare to speak, and spare to speed;
  She'll aiblins listen to my vow: *perhaps*
Should she refuse, I'll lay my dead   *death*
  To her twa een sae bonie blue!

JEAN JAFFREY, the daughter of the Rev. Andrew Jaffrey, minister of Lochmaben Church, Dumfriesshire, was born in 1773. Burns met her in Moffat at the lodgings of his friend, Mr William Nicol, who had gone there for the benefit of his child's health. Jean was only fifteen years of age and Burns seems to

[1] I went woeful away yesterday evening.

95

have been attracted by her extraordinary beauty, her sweet winning manners, her golden tresses and rosy cheeks, and especially 'her twa e'en sae bonie blue'. She seemed to move about with an ease and grace of one much older in years, and Burns was so charmed with her that next morning at the breakfast table he presented her with the song, 'The Blue-e'ed Lassie'. In 1794 Jean married Mr James Renwick, a young Liverpool merchant from New York, U.S.A., and soon accompanied him on his return to the States, and settled there.

Another of Burns's songs, said to be in honour of Jeanie, was first published in the *New York Mirror* in 1846.

When First I saw Fair Jeanie's Face

When first I saw fair Jeanie's face,
　　I couldna tell what ailed me,
My heart went fluttering pit-a-pat,
　　My een they almost failed me.
She's aye sae neat, sae trim, sae tight,　　*so*
　　All grace does round her hover,
Ae look deprived me o' my heart,
　　And I became a lover.

CHORUS

She's aye, aye sae blythe, sae gay,
　　She's aye sae blythe and cheerie;
She's aye sae bonie, blythe, and gay,
　　O gin I were her dearie!　　*if*

Had I Dundas's whole estate,
　　Or Hopetoun's wealth to shine in;
Did warlike laurels crown my brow,
　　Or humbler bays entwining—
I'd lay them a' at Jeanie's feet,
　　Could I but hope to move her,
And prouder than a belted knight,
　　I'd be my Jeanie's lover.
　　　　She's aye, etc.

But sair I fear some happier swain *a rustic lover*
 Has gained sweet Jeanie's favour:
If so, may every bliss be hers,
 Though I maun never have her. *must*
But gang she east, or gang she west, *go*
 'Twixt Forth and Tweed all over,
While men have eyes, or ears, or taste,
 She'll always find a lover.
  She's aye, etc.

In her widowhood she often looked back with a melancholy satisfaction on the many evenings she spent in the company of the great bard in the social circle of her father's fireside, listening to the brilliant sallies of his imagination and to his delightful conversation. 'Many times', she said, 'have I seen Burns enter my father's dwelling on a cold, rainy night, after a long ride over the dreary moors. It was during these visits that he felt himself perfectly happy, and opened his whole soul to us, repeated and even sang many of his admirable songs, and enchanted all who had the good fortune to be present with his manly, luminous observations and artless manners. I never could fancy that Burns had ever followed the rustic occupation of the plough, because everything he said or did had a gracefulness and charm that was in an extraordinary degree engaging.'

Jean died in 1850.

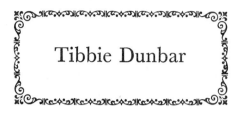

Tibbie Dunbar

1789, age 30

O wilt thou go wi' me, sweet Tibbie Dunbar?
O wilt thou go wi' me, sweet Tibbie Dunbar?
Wilt thou ride on a horse, or be drawn in a car,
Or walk by my side, O sweet Tibbie Dunbar?
I care na thy daddie, his lands and his money,   *care not*
I care na thy kin, sae high and sae lordly;
But say thou wilt hae me for better for waur,   *worse*
And come in thy coatie, sweet Tibbie Dunbar.   *coat*

THIS song was written by Burns to preserve an air he greatly
admired called 'Johnie McGill' after its composer, John McGill,
a Girvan fiddler.

Anna Stewart

1790, age 31

Sweet Anna

Sweet Anna has an air—a grace,
    Divine, magnetic, touching;
She talks, she charms—but who can trace
    The process of bewitching?

Anna's Charms

Anna, thy charms my bosom fire,
    And waste my soul with care;
But ah! how bootless to admire,   *useless*
    When fated to despair!

Yet in thy presence, lovely Fair,
    To hope may be forgiven;
For sure 'twere impious to despair
    So much in sight of Heaven.

Anna was the accomplished daughter of Mr John Stewart of
East Craigs, who had a great friend and correspondent in
Alexander Cunningham, a Writer to the Signet in Edinburgh.
For several years he was passionately but hopelessly in love
with Anna, who apparently did not object to his advances, but
rather encouraged him. Then suddenly she went off with a
richer rival, and on 13th January 1789 married Dr Forrest
Dewar, an Edinburgh surgeon. Cunningham took being thus
jilted sore to heart, and Burns accordingly wrote to him the
following letter:

H   99

'MY DEAR CUNNINGHAM,—When I saw in my last newspaper that a surgeon in Edinburgh was married to a certain amiable and accomplished young lady whose name begins with Anne, a lady with whom, I fancy, I have the honour of being a little acquainted, I sincerely felt for a much-esteemed friend of mine. As you are the single, only instance that ever came within the sphere of my observation of human nature of a young fellow, dissipated, but not debauched, a circumstance that has ever given me the highest idea of the native qualities of your heart, I am certain that a disappointment in the tender passion must to you be a very serious matter.

'To the hopeful youth, keen on the badger foot of Mammon, or listed under the gaudy banners of ambition, a love-disappointment, as such, is an easy business; but to your scanty tribe of mankind, whose souls bear—on the richest materials—the most elegant impress of the great Creator, love enters deeply into their existence—it is entwined with their very thread of life.'

He then composed some verses not very complimentary to Anna, but meant to console the deserted lover.

SHE'S FAIR AND FAUSE

SHE's fair and fause that causes my smart,	*false*
I lo'ed her meikle and lang;	*much; long*
She's broken her vow, she's broken my heart,	
And I may e'en gae hang.	*go*
A coof cam in wi' routh o' gear,	*ninny; plenty of riches*
And I hae tint my dearest dear;	*lost*
But woman is but warld's gear,	
Sae let the bonie lass gang.	*go*

Whae'er ye be that woman love,	
To this be never blind,	
Nae ferlie 'tis tho' fickle she prove,	*no wonder is it*
A woman has't by kind:	*nature*
O woman, lovely woman fair!	
An angel form's faun to thy share,	*fallen*
'Twad been o'er meikle to gien thee mair	*much; have given . . .*
I mean an angel mind.	[*more*

Long after Cunningham himself had been married to another, friends noticed that when he was in Princes Street, Edinburgh, he would pause for a while opposite the house where Anna lived, and gaze up at the window as if anxious to catch a glimpse of her. He seemed to be oblivious to everything else, recollecting the happy times of years gone by, never to return.

Burns also wrote a song, 'Had I a cave on some wild distant shore', of which Chambers says with reference to Anna, who at this time was the widow of Dr Dewar: 'One evening, a few years ago, a friend of mine, visiting a musical family who resided in Princes Street, nearly opposite St John's Chapel, chanced to request one of the young ladies to sing "Had I a Cave, etc." She was about to comply when it was recollected that the heroine of the lyric lived in the flat below, an aged widow, who might overhear it. For that reason the intention of singing the song was laid aside.'

HAD I A CAVE

HAD I a cave on some wild distant shore,
Where the winds howl to the waves' dashing roar;
   There would I weep my woes,
   There seek my lost repose,
   Till grief my eyes should close,
     Ne'er to wake more!

Falsest of womankind! canst thou declare,
All thy fond-plighted vows—fleeting as air?
   To thy new lover hie,
   Laugh o'er thy perjury;
   Then in thy bosom try
     What peace is there?

Anna Park

1790, age 31

SHE is the sunshine o' my e'e,   *eye*
   To live but her I canna;   *cannot*
Had I on earth but wishes three,
   The first would be my Anna.

ANNA PARK, niece of Mrs Hyslop, of the Globe Tavern, Dumfries, was a maidservant in her employment, and made herself very agreeable to customers when serving wines. Burns was a frequent visitor at the Globe, and became too intimate with her, with the result that on 31st March 1791 she became an unmarried mother.

Cunningham speaks of her as a young lady 'with a light foot, and a merry eye', but Thomson regarded her with aversion, and wondered why Burns should have written a song to celebrate such a 'free character'. He was for rejecting it right away, but Burns insisted on its publication, saying: 'I think it is the best love-song I ever composed in my life.' Few, indeed, will agree with Burns about that. Nothing was heard of Anna at any later date, and consequently it is presumed that she died in childbirth. The child was sent first to Mossgiel farm to be cared for and then brought to Ellisland, where the all-too-ready-to-forgive Jean Armour, Burns's wife, took her in, and brought her up as one of her own.

The Gowden Locks of Anna

Yestreen I had a pint o' wine,   *Last night*
   A place where body saw na;
Yestreen lay on this breast o' mine
   The gowden locks of Anna: *golden*
The hungry Jew in wilderness
   Rejoicing o'er his manna,
Was naething to my hinny bliss   *honey*
   Upon the lips of Anna!

Ye monarchs! tak' the east and west,
   Frae Indus to Savannah;
Gi'e me within my straining grasp
   The melting form of Anna!
Then I'll despise imperial charms—
   An empress or sultana;
While dying raptures in her arms,
   I give and take with Anna!

Awa', thou flaunting god o' day!
   Awa', thou pale Diana!
Ilk star gae hide thy twinkling ray,   *each; go*
   When I'm to meet my Anna!
Come, in thy raven plumage, Night!
   Sun, moon, and stars withdraw a'—
And bring an angel pen to write
   My transports wi' my Anna!

Deborah Davies

1791, age 32

THE BONIE WEE THING

CHORUS

Bonie wee thing, cannie wee thing,	*beautiful little;*
Lovely wee thing, wert thou mine,	[*gentle*
I would wear thee in my bosom,	
Lest my jewel I should tine!	*lose*

WISHFULLY I look and languish,
  In that bonie face o' thine;
And my heart it stounds wi' anguish,   *aches*
  Lest my wee thing be na mine.
  — *Bonie wee,* etc.

Wit, and Grace, and Love, and Beauty,
  In ae constellation shine;   *one*
To adore thee is my duty,
  Goddess o' this soul o' mine!
  Bonie wee, etc.

THE heroine of this popular song was Miss Deborah Davies, the youngest daughter of Dr Davies of Tenby in Pembrokeshire. She was connected by ties of blood with the family of Captain Riddel of Glenriddel, at whose house Burns probably first met her. Her education was superior to that of most young ladies of her station of life; she was equally agreeable and witty; her company was much courted in Nithsdale, and others than

Burns respected her talents in poetic composition. She was then in her twentieth year, and so little and so handsome that some-one who desired to compliment her welcomed her to the Vale of Nith as one of the Graces in miniature. Her beauty and accomplishments appear to have made a deep impression upon Burns, for he has celebrated them in a number of effusions in both prose and verse. In a letter to her enclosing the undernoted song, he says, in a strain of enthusiastic gallantry: 'When my theme is youth and beauty—a young lady whose personal charms, wit, and sentiment are equally striking and unaffected —by Heavens! though I had lived three-score years a married man, and three-score years before I was a married man, my imagination would hallow the very idea; and I am truly sorry that the enclosed stanzas have done such poor justice to such a subject.'

LOVELY DAVIES

O HOW shall I, unskilfu', try
    The poet's occupation—
The tunefu' powers, in happy hours,
    That whisper inspiration?
Even they maun dare an effort mair,   *must; more*
    Than aught they ever gave us,
Ere they rehearse, in equal verse,
    The charms o' lovely Davies.

Each eye it cheers when she appears,
    Like Phoebus in the morning—
When past the show'r, and every flower
    The garden is adorning.
As the wretch looks o'er Siberia's shore,
    When winter-bound the wave is;
Sae droops our heart when we maun part
    Frae charming, lovely Davies.

Her smile's a gift frae 'boon the lift,   *above heaven*
    That maks us mair than princes—
A scepter'd hand—a king's command,
    Is in her darting glances:

The man in arms 'gainst female charms,
   Even he her willing slave is;
He hugs his chain, and owns the reign
   Of conquering, lovely Davies.

My Muse to dream of such a theme,
   Her feeble powers surrender;
The eagle's gaze alone surveys
   The sun's meridian splendour:
I wad in vain essay the strain,   *would*
   The deed too daring brave is;
I'll drap the lyre, and mute, admire,   *drop*
   The charms o' lovely Davies.

In August 1791 Burns wrote to Miss Davies: 'Woman is the blood-royal of life; let them be all sacred. Whether this last sentiment be right or wrong, I am not accountable; it is an original component feature of my mind.'

Allan Cunningham writes: 'One day, while Burns was at Moffat, the charming, lovely Davies rode past, accompanied by a lady tall and portly; on a friend asking the poet why God made one lady so large and Miss Davies so little, he replied at once in the epigram:

Ask why God made the gem so small,
   And why so huge the granite?—
Because God meant mankind should set
   The higher value on it.

This impromptu was afterwards written by the poet on a window pane of the Black Bull Inn at Moffat, but the piece of glass which it emblazoned has long since disappeared.

According to Cunningham also: 'It was the destiny of Miss Davies to become acquainted with Captain Delany, a pleasant and sightly man, who made himself acceptable to her by sympathizing in her pursuits, and by writing verses to her, calling her his "Stella"—an ominous name, which might have brought the memory of Swift's unhappy mistress to her mind. An offer of marriage was made and accepted; but Delany's circumstances were urged as an obstacle; delays ensued: a coldness on the lover's part followed; his regiment was called abroad—he went with it; she heard from him once and no more, and was left to mourn the change of affection—to droop and die. He perished in battle, or by a foreign climate, soon after the death of the young lady of whose love he was unworthy.'

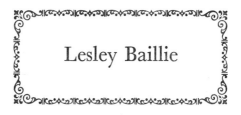

Lesley Baillie

1792, age 33

BONIE LESLEY

O, saw ye bonie Lesley,
  As she gaed ower the Border?   *went over*
She's gane, like Alexander,
  To spread her conquests farther.

To see her is to love her,
  And love but her for ever;
For nature made her what she is,
  And never made anither!

Thou art a queen, fair Lesley,
  Thy subjects we, before thee;
Thou art divine, fair Lesley,
  The hearts o' men adore thee.

The deil he couldna skaith thee,   *devil; harm*
  Or aught that wad belang thee;   *would belong to*
He'd look into thy bonie face,
  And say, 'I canna wrang thee!'   *wrong*

The powers aboon will tent thee,   *above; guard*
  Misfortune sha' na steer thee;   *molest*
Thou'rt like themselves sae lovely,
  That ill they'll ne'er let near thee.

> Return again, fair Lesley,
>   Return to Caledonie!
> That we may brag, we hae a lass   *boast*
>   There's nane again sae bonie.

IN a letter to Mrs Dunlop, Burns gives the following account of the origin of this song: 'Apropos!—do you know that I am almost in love with an acquaintance of yours? Know then that the heart-struck awe, the distant humble approach, the delight we should have in gazing upon and listening to a messenger of Heaven, appearing in all the unspotted purity of his celestial home, among the coarse, polluted, far inferior sons of men, to deliver to them tidings that make their hearts swim in joy, and their imaginations soar in transport—such, so delighting and so pure, were the emotions of my soul on meeting the other day with Miss Lesley Baillie, your neighbour, at Mayfield. Mr B. with his two daughters, accompanied by Mr H. of G., passing through Dumfries a few days ago, on their way to England, did me the honour of calling on me; on which I took my horse, (though God knows I could ill spare the time,) and accompaned them fourteen or fifteen miles, and dined and spent the day with them. 'Twas about nine, I think, when I left them, and, riding home, I composed the following ballad, of which you will probably think you have a dear bargain, as it will cost you another groat of postage. You must know that there is an old ballad beginning with—

> My bonie Lizzie Baillie,
> I'll rowe thee in my plaidie, etc.

So I parodied it as follows, which is literally the first copy, "unanointed, unanneal'd," as Hamlet says—

> O, saw ye bonie Lesley
>   As she gaed o'er the Border?
> She's gane, like Alexander,
>   To spread her conquests farther.'

A year after he had composed 'Bonie Lesley', so sensitive was he to feminine beauty that he wrote another in her honour.

Blythe hae I been

Blythe hae I been on yon hill,
  As the lambs before me;
Careless ilka thought and free,   *every*
  As the breeze flew o'er me,
Now nae langer sport and play,   *no longer*
  Mirth or sang can please me;
Lesley is sae fair and coy,
  Care and anguish seize me.

Heavy, heavy is the task,
  Hopeless love declaring:
Trembling, I dow nocht but glower,   *can do nothing; stare*
  Sighing, dumb, despairing!
If she winna ease the throes   *will not; throes*
  In my bosom swelling;
Underneath the grass-green sod,
  Soon maun be my dwelling.   *must*

He was surely in an ecstatic mood over this incomparable young lady when he describes this song as 'one of the finest songs ever I made in my life; and besides is composed on a young lady, positively the most beautiful, lovely woman in the world'.

In 'Bonie Lesley', verses 4 and 5, we have Burns's idea of human female loveliness indicating goodness and resembling the divine nature or celestial powers; and by its resemblance propitiating their favour. It grows naturally out of his profound devotion to beauty, and enables him to interpret after a most instructive and characteristic fashion the love for loveliness in the divine nature. Scholars are agreed that Burns accepted this as a supreme law in the universe and that he could believe in no sort of doctrine, moral or theological, that was opposed to it.

In 1799 Lesley married Mr Robert Cumming of Logie and died in Edinburgh in July 1843.

Jane Blackstock

1793, age 34

O Poortith Cauld

O POORTITH cauld, and restless love,   *cold poverty*
  Ye wreck my peace between ye;
Yet poortith a' I could forgive,
  An 'twere na for my Jeanie.

CHORUS

O why should Fate sic pleasure have,   *such*
  Life's dearest bands untwining?
Or why sae sweet a flower as love,
  Depend on Fortune's shining.

This warld's wealth, when I think on,
  Its pride, and a' the lave o't;   *rest of it*
Fie, fie on silly coward man
  That he should be the slave o't!
    O why, etc.

Her een sae bonie blue, betray   *eyes*
  How she repays my passion;
But prudence is her o'erword aye,   *refrain*
  She talks of rank and fashion.
    O why, etc.

O wha can prudence think upon,
  And sic a lassie by him?   *such*
O wha can prudence think upon,
  And sae in love as I am?
    O why, etc.

111

> How blest the humble cotter's fate!
>   He wooes his simple dearie;   *courts*
> The silly bogles, wealth and state,
>   Can never make them eerie.   *afraid*
>   *O why*, etc.

GILBERT BURNS says that a Miss Jane Blackstock, who afterwards became Mrs Whittier of Liverpool, was the heroine of this
song. The poet, in a letter to Thomson, said: 'For private
reasons, I should like to see it in print.'

The reasons Burns had for this are not known. The song seems
to suggest that it was a case of ill-requited love, Jane preferring
rank and fashion to that of becoming a poor ploughman's wife.

Here is the poet's first song to Jeanie when he was in love with
her. The last eight lines had already appeared in his song
'Bonie Peggy Alison'.

COME, LET ME TAKE THEE TO MY BREAST

> COME, let me take thee to my breast,
>   And pledge we ne'er shall sunder;
> And I shall spurn as vilest dust
>   The warld's wealth and grandeur:
> And do I hear my Jeanie own
>   That equal transports move her?
> I ask for dearest life alone
>   That I may live to love her.
>
> Thus in my arms, wi' all thy charms,
>   I clasp my countless treasure;
> I'll seek nae mair o' heaven to share,
>   Than sic a moment's pleasure: *such*
> And by thy een sae bonie blue   *eyes*
>   I sware I'm thine for ever!
> And on thy lips I seal my vow,
>   And break it shall I never!

Jean Lorimer
(*Chloris*)

1793, age 34

WHISTLE, AND I'LL COME TO YOU, MY LAD

CHORUS

O whistle, and I'll come to you, my lad,
O whistle, and I'll come to you, my lad;
Though father and mither and a' should gae mad,   *go*
O whistle, and I'll come to you, my lad.

BUT warily tent, when ye come to court me,	*cautiously; heed*
And come na unless the back-yett be a-jee;	*not; private gate ajar*
Syne up the back-stile, and let naebody see,	*then*
And come as ye were na comin' to me.	*not*
O whistle, etc.	

At kirk, or at market, whene'er ye meet me,	
Gang by me as though that ye cared nae a flie;	*go; not a fly*
But steal me a blink o' your bonie black e'e,	*glance; eye*
Yet look as ye were na lookin' at me.	
O whistle, etc.	

Aye vow and protest that ye care na for me,	
And whiles ye may lightly my beauty a wee;	*think lightly of; little*
But court na anither, though jokin' ye be,	
For fear that she wile your fancy frae me.	*beguile*
O whistle, etc.	

In his letter to Mr G. Thomson, Burns writes: 'In "Whistle and I'll come to ye, my lad", the iteration of that line is tiresome to my ear. Here goes what I think is an improvement:

113

O whistle, and I'll come to ye, my lad,
O whistle, and I'll come to ye, my lad;
Though father, and mother, and a' should gae mad,
Thy Jeanie will venture wi' ye, my lad.

'In fact, a fair dame, at whose shrine I, the Priest of the Nine,
offer up the incense of Parnassus; a dame whom the Graces have
attired in witchcraft, and whom the Loves have armed with
lightning; a fair one, herself the heroine of the song, insists on
the amendment, and dispute her commands if you dare!' In
reply from Edinburgh, 3rd August 1795, Mr Thomson says:
'I am sorry you should be induced to alter "O whistle, and
I'll come to ye, my lad", to the prosaic line, "Thy Jeanie will
venture wi' ye, my lad". I must be permitted to say that I do
not think the latter either reads or sings so well as the former.
I wish, therefore, you would, in my name, petition the charming
Jeanie, whosoever she be, to let the line remain unaltered.' The
new verse appeared in the second edition of the songs, but future
editions reverted to the original.

The heroine of the song was Jean Lorimer, the 'Lassie wi' the
Lint-white Locks'. The fact is that Burns was no sooner off
with one charmer than he was on with a new one. Dr Cairns
says that he heard Jean Lorimer 'sing the song herself in the
very spirit of arch-simplicity which it requires'.

Jean was born at Craigieburn, a mansion of picturesque
beauty near Moffat. Her father, Mr William Lorimer, had a
prosperous farm on the banks of the Nith, near Dumfries. The
poet was on terms of the closest intimacy with him. Here he
first saw and admired this charming creature who, though only
seventeen, was now in the full bloom of her dazzling beauty, and
destined to task his Muse to its highest heaven of invention. She
had, of course, no lack of suitors, many of whom were men of
worth and honour; but unfortunately for herself her choice fell
upon a showy, heartless impostor of the name of Whelpdale, a
native of the county of Cumberland, who had settled as a farmer
in the neighbourhood of Moffat and with whom she eloped one
night from her father's house to Gretna Green, where they were
married. A few short months after this romantic affair, he

husband, who was naturally of reckless and extravagant habits, fled from the district to avoid his creditors, leaving his wife to return to her father's without a penny to support her. Jean spent her last days in the neighbourhood of Edinburgh and died in September 1831. She was interred in Newington churchyard. Her grave is marked by a memorial stone erected in 1901 by the Edinburgh Ninety Burns Club.

Burns seems at first to have had a platonic love for 'Chloris'— an Arcadian name he gave to Jean before her marriage to Whelpdale—and she at first seems to have loved him, as witness the following song:

She says she Lo'es me Best of A'

Sae flaxen were her ringlets,	*so*
Her eyebrows of a darker hue,	
Bewitchingly o'er-arching	
Twa laughing een o' bonie blue.	*eyes*
Her smiling, sae wyling,	*so enticing*
Wad make a wretch forget his woe!	*would*
What pleasure, what treasure,	
Unto those rosy lips to grow!	
Such was my Chloris' bonie face,	
When first her bonie face I saw;	
And ay my Chloris' dearest charm,	
She says she lo'es me best of a'!	

Like harmony her motion,	
Her pretty ankle is a spy,	
Betraying fair proportion,	
Wad make a saint forget the sky!	*would*
Sae warming, sae charming,	
Her fautless form and gracefu' air,	*faultless*
Ilk feature—auld Nature	*each*
Declar'd that she could do nae mair!	*no more*
Hers are the willing chains o' love,	
By conquering beauty's sovereign law;	
And ay my Chloris' dearest charm,	
She says she lo'es me best of a'!	

I

Let others love the city,
   And gaudy show at sunny noon;
Gi'e me the lonely valley,
   The dewy eve, and rising moon:
Fair beaming, and streaming,
   Her silver light the boughs amang;
While falling, recalling,
   The amorous thrush concludes his sang;
There, dearest Chloris, wilt thou rove
   By wimpling burn and leafy shaw,   *meandering;*
And hear my vows o' truth and love,   [*grove*
   And say thou lo'es me best of a'?

On the panes of glass in the Globe Inn, Dumfries, Burns was
frequently in the habit of writing many of his witty *jeux d'esprit,*
as well as fragmentary portions of his most celebrated songs. We
fear these precious relics have now been wholly abstracted by
the lovers and collectors of literary rarities. John Speirs, Esq., of
Elderslie, had in his possession one of these panes of glass, upon
which is written in Burns's autograph the following verse of
'Sae flaxen were her ringlets':

Hers are the willing chains o' love,
   By conquering beauty's sovereign law;
And ay my Chloris' dearest charm,
   She says she lo'es me best of a'!

Burns wrote many other songs of which Chloris was the
subject. The following are the best known:

It was the Charming Month of May

It was the charming month of May,
When all the flowers were fresh and gay,
One morning, by the break of day,
   The youthful, charming Chloe—
From peaceful slumber she arose,
Girt on her mantle and her hose,
And o'er the flowery mead she goes,
   The youthful, charming Chloe.

CHORUS

Lovely was she by the dawn,
Youthful Chloe, charming Chloe,
Tripping o'er the pearly lawn,
The youthful, charming Chloe.

The feathered people, you might see
Perched all around on every tree,
In notes of sweetest melody
  They hail the charming Chloe;
Till, painting gay the eastern skies,
The glorious sun began to rise,
Out-rivalled by the radiant eyes
  Of youthful, charming Chloe.
    Lovely was she, etc.

'The following song', says the poet, 'has at least the merit of being a regular pastoral: the vernal morn, the summer noon, the autumnal evening, and the winter night, are regularly rounded. The air puts me in raptures; and, in fact, unless I be pleased with the tune, I never can make verses to it.'

LASSIE WI' THE LINT-WHITE LOCKS

CHORUS

Lassie wi' the lint-white locks,   *flaxen colour*
  Bonie lassie, artless lassie,
Wilt thou wi' me tent the flocks?   *attend to*
  Wilt thou be my dearie O?

Now nature cleeds the flowery lea,   *clothes*
And a' is young and sweet like thee;
O wilt thou share its joys wi' me,
  And say thou'lt be my dearie O?
    Lassie wi', etc.

And when the welcome simmer-shower
Has cheer'd ilk drooping little flower;   *each*
We'll to the breathing woodbine bower
  At sultry moon, my dearie O.
    Lassie wi', etc.

When Cynthia lights, wi' silver ray,
The weary shearer's hameward way;   *reapers*
Thro' yellow waving fields we'll stray,
    And talk o' love, my dearie O.
     Lassie wi', etc.

And when the howling wintry blast
Disturbs my lassie's midnight rest;
Enclaspèd to my faithfu' breast,
    I'll comfort thee, my dearie O.
     Lassie wi', etc.

Mark Yonder Pomp of Costly Fashion

Mark yonder pomp of costly fashion,
    Round the wealthy titled bride;
But when compar'd with real passion,
    Poor is all that princely pride:
    What are their showy treasures?
    What are their noisy pleasures?
The gay, gaudy glare of vanity and art:
    The polish'd jewel's blaze,
    May draw the wond'ring gaze,
    And courtly grandeur bright,
    The fancy may delight,
But never, never can come near the heart.

But did you see my dearest Chloris,
    In simplicity's array;
Lovely as yon sweet opening flower is,
    Shrinking from the gaze of day;
    O then, the heart alarming,
    And all resistless charming,
In love's delightful fetters she chains the willing soul!
    Ambition would disown
    The world's imperial crown,
    Even Av'rice would deny
    His worship'd deity,
And feel thro' every vein love's raptures roll.

The following song was sent to Jean Lorimer but was meant
by Burns to be a compliment to Jean Armour.

No my Ain Lassie

CHORUS

O this is no my ain lassie,   own
 Fair though the lassie be;
O weel ken I my ain lassie,   well know
 Kind love is in her e'e.   eye

I SEE a form, I see a face,
Ye weel may wi' the fairest place;
It wants, to me, the witching grace,—
 The kind love that's in her e'e.
  O this is no, etc.

She's bonie, blooming, straight, and tall,
And lang has had my heart in thrall; enslaved
And aye it charms my very saul,— soul
 The kind love that's in her e'e.
  O this is no, etc.

A thief sae pawkie is my Jean,   cunning
To steal a blink, by a' unseen;
But gleg as light are lovers' een, sharp, quick; eyes
 When kind love is in the e'e.
  O this is no, etc.

It may escape the courtly sparks,
It may escape the learnèd clerks;
But weel the watching lover marks well
 The kind love that's in her e'e. eye
  O this is no, etc.

I'll Ay Ca' In by Yon Town

CHORUS

I'll ay ca' in by yon town,   call; hamlet
 And by yon garden green, again;
I'll ay ca' in by yon town,
 And see my bonie Jean again.
There's nane sall ken, there's nane sall guess, none shall know
 What brings me back the gate again, same way
But she my fairest faithfu' lass,
 And stow'nlins we sall meet again. by stealth
  I'll aye ca' in, etc.

She'll wander by the aiken tree,   *oak*
  When trystin time draws near again; *love meeting time*
And when her lovely form I see,
  O haith, she's doubly dear again!   *faith*
    I'll aye ca' in, etc.

Their Groves o' Sweet Myrtle

THEIR groves o' sweet myrtle let foreign lands reckon,
  Where bright-beaming summers exalt the perfume;
Far dearer to me yon lone glen o' green breckan,
  Wi' the burn stealing under the lang yellow broom.   *long*

Far dearer to me are yon humble broom bowèrs,
  Where the blue-bell and gowan lurk lowly unseen;
For there, lightly tripping amang the wild-flowèrs,
  A-listening the linnet, aft wanders my Jean.   *oft*

Though rich is the breeze in their gay sunny valleys,
  And cauld Caledonia's blast on the wave;
Their sweet-scented woodlands that skirt the proud palace,
  What are they?—the haunt of the tyrant and slave!

The slave's spicy forests, and gold-bubbling fountains,
  The brave Caledonian views wi' disdain;
He wanders as free as the winds of his mountains,
  Save love's willing fetters—the chains of his Jean!

Oh, Bonie was yon Rosy Brier

OH, bonie was yon rosy brier,
  That blooms sae far frae haunt o' man;
And bonie she, and ah, how dear!
  It shaded frae the e'enin' sun.

Yon rosebuds in the morning dew,
  How pure amang the leaves sae green;
But purer was the lover's vow
  They witness'd in their shade yestreen.   *last night*

All in its rude and prickly bower,
   That crimson rose, how sweet and fair!
But love is far a sweeter flower
   Amid life's thorny path o' care.

The pathless wild and wimpling burn,   *meandering*
   Wi' Chloris in my arms, be mine;
And I the world, nor wish, nor scorn,
   Its joys and griefs alike resign.

'TWAS NA HER BONIE BLUE E'E

'TWAS na her bonie blue e'e was my ruin;   *not; eye*
Fair tho' she be, that was ne'er my undoing:
'Twas the dear smile when naebody did mind us,
'Twas the bewitching, sweet, stown glance o' kindness. *stealthy*

Sair do I fear that to hope is denied me,   *sore*
Sair do I fear that despair maun abide me;   *must*
But tho' fell fortune should fate us to sever,
Queen shall she be in my bosom for ever.

Chloris, I'm thine wi' a passion sincerest,
And thou hast plighted me love o' the dearest!
And thou'rt the angel that never can alter,
Sooner the sun in his motion would falter.

O WHA IS SHE THAT LO'ES ME?

O WHA is she that lo'es me,
   And has my heart a-keeping?
O sweet is she that lo'es me,
   As dews o' simmer weeping,   *summer*
   In tears the rose-buds steeping!

CHORUS

O that's the lassie o' my heart,
   My lassie ever dearer;
O that's the queen o' womankind,
   And ne'er a ane to peer her.   *one*

If thou shalt meet a lassie
  In grace and beauty charming,
That e'en thy chosen lassie,
  Erewhile thy breast sae warming,
  Had ne'er sic powers alarming;   *such*
    O that's the lassie, etc.

If thou hadst heard her talking—
  And thy attentions plighted,
That ilka body talking,   *every*
  But her by thee is slighted—
  And thou art all delighted;
    O that's the lassie, etc.

If thou hast met this fair one;
  When frae her thou hast parted,   *from*
If every other fair one,
  But her, thou hast deserted,
  And thou art broken-hearted;
    O that's the lassie, etc.

Craigieburn Wood

Sweet fa's the eve on Craigieburn,
  And blythe awakes the morrow,
But a' the pride o' Spring's return
  Can yield me nocht but sorrow.   *nothing*

I see the flowers and spreading trees,
  I hear the wild birds singing;
But what a weary wight can please,
  And Care his bosom is wringing?

Fain, fain would I my griefs impart,
  Yet dare na for your anger;
But secret love will break my heart,
  If I conceal it langer.

If thou refuse to pity me,
  If thou shalt love another,
When yon green leaves fade frae the tree,
  Around my grave they'll wither.

Regarding the following song, the poet says: 'Having been on a visit the other day to my fair Chloris—that is the poetic name of the lovely goddess of my inspiration—she suggested an idea, which, on my return home, I wrought into the following song':

CHLORIS

My Chloris, mark how green the groves,
    The primrose banks how fair;
The balmy gales awake the flowers,
    And wave thy flaxen hair.

The laverock shuns the palace gay,   *lark*
    And o'er the cottage sings;
For nature smiles as sweet, I ween,   *fancy*
    To shepherds as to kings.

Let minstrels sweep the skilfu' string
    In lordly lighted ha';   *hall*
The shepherd stops his simple reed,
    Blythe, in the birken shaw.   *birchen-
        wood*

The princely revel may survey
    Our rustic dance wi' scorn;
But are their hearts as light as ours,
    Beneath the milk-white thorn?

The shepherd in the flowery glen,
    In shepherd's phrase will woo;   *court*
The courtier tells a finer tale—
    But is his heart as true?

These wild-wood flowers I've pu'd, to deck   *pulled*
    That spotless breast o' thine;
The courtier's gems may witness love—
    But 'tisna love like mine.

'Ah, Chloris' was written at the time when Miss Lorimer was induced to form the matrimonial connection with Whelpdale. In these circumstances the language of the poet-lover seems appropriate and natural. The first and last verses are especially beautiful.

AH, CHLORIS, SINCE IT MAY NA BE

Ah, Chloris, since it may na be,   *not*
　　That thou of love wilt hear;
If from the lover thou maun flee,   *must*
　　Yet let the *friend* be dear.

Altho' I love my Chloris mair   *more*
　　Than ever tongue could tell;
My passion I will ne'er declare,
　　I'll say, I wish thee well.

Tho' a' my daily care thou art,
　　And a' my nightly dream,
I'll hide the struggle in my heart,
　　And say it is esteem.

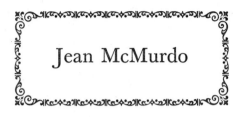

Jean McMurdo

1793, age 34

' I HAVE just finished the following ballad,' says the poet to
Thomson, 'and as I do think it is in my best style, I send it to
you.' The heroine of this song was Miss Jane McMurdo, the
eldest daughter of John McMurdo, Esq., chamberlain to the
Duke of Queensberry, and who resided, with a family of charming and accomplished daughters, at the ducal seat of Drumlanrig, a few miles from the poet's farm. A frequent guest at this
gentleman's table, he appears to have lived on terms of intimacy
with the entire family. 'The heroine', he tells us, 'I did not
paint in the rank which she held in life; but in the dress and
character of a cottager; consequently the utmost simplicity of
thought and expression was necessary. . . . Mr Clarke, who
wrote down the air from Mrs Burns's "woodnotes wild", is
very fond of it, and has given it a celebrity by teaching it to
some young ladies of fashion here.' And sending the ballad to
Jean McMurdo, Burns says: 'In the enclosed ballad I have, I
think, hit off a few outlines of your portrait. The *naïveté* of heart
and manners in my heroine are, I flatter myself, a pretty just
likeness of Miss McMurdo in a cottage.'

BONIE JEAN

THERE was a lass and she was fair,
    At kirk and market to be seen;
When a' the fairest maids were met,
    The fairest maid was bonie Jean:

125

And ay she wrought her mammie's wark,   *mother's work*
   And ay she sang sae merrilie;
The blythest bird upon the bush,
   Had ne'er a lighter heart than she.

But hawks will rob the tender joys
   That bless the little lintwhite's nest;   *linnet*
And frost will blight the fairest flowers,
   And love will break the soundest rest.
Young Robie was the brawest lad,
   The flower and pride of a' the glen;
And he had owsen, sheep, and kye,   *oxen; cows*
   And wanton naigies nine or ten: *young horses*

He gaed wi' Jeanie to the tryste,   *went; fair, lover's meeting*
   He danc'd wi' Jeanie on the down;   [*place*
And lang e'er witless Jeanie wist,   *long*
   Her heart was tint, her peace was stown. *lost; stolen*
As in the bosom o' the stream,
   The moon-beam dwells at dewy e'en;   *evening*
So trembling, pure, was tender love
   Within the breast o' bonie Jean.

And now she works her mammie's wark,
   And ay she sighs wi' care and pain;
Ye wist na what her ail might be,
   Or what wad mak' her weel again.   *well*
But did na Jeanie's heart loup light,   *leap*
   And did na joy blink in her e'e,   *sparkle—a smiling look*
As Robie tauld a tale o' love   *told*
   Ae e'enin' on the lily lea?

The sun was sinking in the west,
   The birds sang sweet in ilka grove;   *every*
His cheek to hers he fondly prest,
   And whisper'd thus his tale o' love:
'O Jeanie fair, I lo'e thee dear;
   O canst thou think to fancy me?
Or wilt thou leave thy mammie's cot,   *mother's*
   And learn to tent the farms wi' me?   *attend*

'At barn or byre thou shalt na drudge,   *not*
 Or naething else to trouble thee;
But stray amang the heather-bells,
 And tent the waving corn wi' me.'   *watch over*
Now what could artless Jeanie do?
 She had nae will to say him na: *no*
At length she blush'd a sweet consent,
 And love was ay between them twa.   *two*

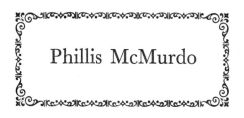

Phillis McMurdo

1793, age 34

MISS PHILADELPHIA MCMURDO was the younger daughter of John McMurdo, a sister of Jean. She was noted in Drumlanrig for her beauty, and Burns sang of her charms in his songs:

PHILLIS THE QUEEN O' THE FAIR

ADOWN winding Nith I did wander,
  To mark the sweet flowers as they spring;
Adown winding Nith I did wander,
  Of Phillis to muse and to sing.

CHORUS

Awa' wi' your belles and your beauties,
  They never wi' her can compare:
Whaever has met wi' my Phillis,
  Has met wi' the queen o' the fair.

The daisy amus'd my fond fancy,
  So artless, so simple, so wild;
Thou emblem, said I, o' my Phillis,
  For she is simplicity's child.
    Awa', etc.

The rose-bud's the blush o' my charmer,
  Her sweet balmy lip when 'tis prest:
How fair and how pure is the lily,
  But fairer and purer her breast.
    Awa', etc.

128

Yon knot of gay flowers in the arbour,
   They ne'er wi' my Phillis can vie:
Her breath is the breath o' the woodbine,
   Its dew-drop o' diamond, her eye.
     Awa', etc.

Her voice is the song of the morning,
   That wakes thro' the green-spreading grove,
When Phoebus peeps over the mountains,
   On music, and pleasure, and love.
     Awa', etc.

But beauty, how frail and how fleeting,
   The bloom of a fine summer's day!
While worth in the mind o' my Phillis
   Will flourish without a decay.
     Awa', etc.

PHILLIS THE FAIR

WHILE larks with little wing
   Fann'd the pure air,
Tasting the breathing spring,
   Forth I did fare:
Gay the sun's golden eye
Peep'd o'er the mountains high;
Such thy morn! did I cry,
   Phillis the fair.

In each bird's careless song
   Glad did I share;
While yon wild flowers among,
   Chance led me there:
Sweet to the opening day
Rosebuds bent the dewy spray;
Such thy bloom! did I say,
   Phillis the fair.

Down in a shady walk
   Doves cooing were;
I mark'd the cruel hawk
   Caught in a snare:

So kind may Fortune be,
Such make his destiny!
He who would injure thee,
    Phillis the fair.

Phillis married Mr Norman Lockhart of Carnwath.

The above song, 'Phillis the Fair', is said to have been written by Burns at the request of his friend, Stephen Clarke, the music master, who taught Phillis music, and was on the way to falling in love with her. Burns, however, was not over-enamoured with either the song or the tune, 'Robin Adair', to which it was set.

MARGARET CHALMERS
(*Page 84*)

ELIZABETH BURNET

(*Page 90*)

Jessie Staig

1793, age 34

Young Jessie

True-hearted was he, the sad swain o' the Yarrow,
　And fair are the maids on the banks o' the Ayr,
But by the sweet side o' the Nith's winding river,
　Are lovers as faithful, and maidens as fair:
To equal young Jessie seek Scotland all over;
　To equal young Jessie you seek it in vain;
Grace, beauty, and elegance fetter her lover,
　And maidenly modesty fixes the chain.

Oh, fresh is the rose in the gay, dewy morning,
　And sweet is the lily at evening close;
But in the fair presence o' lovely young Jessie,
　Unseen is the lily, unheeded the rose.
Love sits in her smile, a wizard ensnaring,
　Enthron'd in her een he delivers his law;
But still to her charms she alone is a stranger;
　Her modest demeanour's the jewel of a'!

This song was written by Burns in 1793 in honour of Miss Jessie Staig, second daughter of the Provost of Dumfries. 'Lovely young Jessie' so captivated the poet, that for grace, beauty and elegance her equal, he declared, could not be found anywhere in Scotland!

One day, on visiting Jessie, he learned that she had just recovered from a fever. In a letter to Thomson he says: 'Doctor Maxwell was the physician who seemingly saved her from the grave, and to him I address the following:

Maxwell, if merit here you crave,
That merit I deny;
You save fair Jessie from the grave?
An angel could not die.'

Jessie married Major William Miller, one of the sons of the poet's former landlord. She died in 1801 and was long remembered for her personal charm and gentleness!

Janet Miller

1794, age 35

Wilt thou be my Dearie?

Wilt thou be my dearie?
When sorrow wrings thy gentle heart.
Wilt thou let me cheer thee?
By the treasure of my soul,
That's the love I bear thee!
I swear and vow that only thou
Shall ever be my dearie.
Only thou, I swear and vow,
Shall ever be my dearie.

Lassie, say thou lo'es me;
Or, if thou wilt na be my ain,   *own*
Say na thou'lt refuse me:
If it winna, canna be,   *will not*
Thou, for thine may choose me,
Let me, lassie, quickly die,
Trusting that thou lo'es me.
Lassie, let me quickly die,
Trusting that thou lo'es me.

THERE is some dubiety about the heroine of this song.
Cunningham tells us that it was composed by Burns during a
brief courtship of Janet Miller of Dalswinton, but it was not
published until 1794.

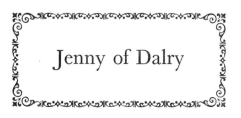

Jenny of Dalry

1794, age 35

COMIN' THRO' THE RYE

COMIN' thro' the rye, poor body,
   Comin' thro' the rye;
She draigl't a' her petticoatie,   *draggled*
   Comin' thro' the rye.

CHORUS

Oh, Jenny's a' weet, poor body,   *wet*
   Jenny's seldom dry;
She draigl't a' her petticoatie,
   Comin' thro' the rye.

Gin a body meet a body   *should*
   Comin' thro' the rye;
Gin a body kiss a body,
   Need a body cry?
     Oh, Jenny's a' weet, etc.

Gin a body meet a body
   Comin' thro' the glen;
Gin a body kiss a body,
   Need the warld ken?
     Oh, Jenny's a' weet, etc.

THERE have been many conjectures about this song. Some artists have pictured Jenny as walking through a field of rye, but it is not at all likely that 'a' her petticoatie' would get bespattered in such a venture, and as the poet points out, Jenny was 'seldom dry'. Others consider that the 'rye' was a long, narrow, winding lane of cobble-stones leading to the town, and especially in wet weather there were many pools of muddy water in it, so that Jenny often had a 'draggled petticoatie'. Sometimes she would 'meet a body' in the lane, and at the corner a number of lads stood who smiled on her! Another consideration which seems more probable is that connected with the Rye. The Rye Water has its source among high hills, past the north-west end of the parish. On its course of eight miles to the Garnock there is a spot where it was crossed by a ford below Ryefield House. Before the erection of any bridge at Drakemire —a suburb of Dalry—the fording of the stream caused much fun and banter, and Burns, it is claimed, immortalized the primitive scene in his song, 'Comin' thro' the rye'. The only objection to this is that Burns does not spell rye with a capital letter.

The words for the Scottish melody sung today are:

Gin a body meet a body
  Comin' through the rye;
Gin a body kiss a body—
  Need a body cry?

CHORUS

Ilka lassie has her laddie,
  Nane they say ha'e I;
Yet a' the lads they smile at me
  When comin' thro' the rye,

Gin a body meet a body
  Comin' frae the town,
Gin a body greet a body,
  Need a body frown.
    Ilka lassie, etc.

Amang the train there is a swain
  I dearly lo'e mysel';
But whaur his hame, or what his name,
  I dinna care to tell.
    Ilka lassie, etc.

There is an additional verse said to have been inscribed by Burns on the window pane of a tavern:

> Gin a body kiss a body
> Comin' through the grain,
> Need a body grudge a body
> What's a body's ain?

This verse, however, is now regarded as spurious. It was Burns's habit in such writing to copy one of the verses from his original song. The verse is most likely to have been the work of some wag imitating Burns, and using the word 'grain' to rhyme with 'ain'. The verse, of course, was meant to support the view that the song refers to a field of rye.

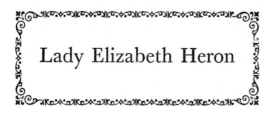

Lady Elizabeth Heron

1794, age 35

HERE IS THE GLEN

HERE is the glen, and here the bower,
  All underneath the birchen shade;
The village-bell has tolled the hour—
  O what can stay my lovely maid?

'Tis not Maria's whispering call;
  'Tis but the balmy-breathing gale,
Mixed with some warbler's dying fall,
  The dewy star of eve to hail.

It is Maria's voice I hear!—
  So calls the woodlark in the grove,
His little faithful mate to cheer;
  At once 'tis music and 'tis love.

And art thou come?—and art thou true?
  O welcome, dear, to love and me!
And let us all our vows renew,
  Along the flow'ry banks of Cree.

LADY HERON (the Maria of the song), apparently had composed an air entitled 'The Banks of Cree', in praise of the beautiful and romantic river of that name. Burns seems to have been enamoured with it. 'I have written the following song to it,' he says, 'as her ladyship is a particular friend of mine.'

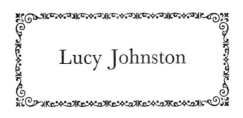

Lucy Johnston

1795, age 36

O Wat ye wha's in Yon Town

CHORUS

O wat ye wha's in yon town,   know
  Ye see the e'ening sun upon?   evening
The dearest maid's in yon town,
  That e'ening sun is shining on.

Now haply down yon gay green shaw,   wood
  She wanders by yon spreading tree;
How blest ye flowers that round her blaw, *blow*
  Ye catch the glances o' her e'e!   eye
    O wat ye wha's, etc.

How blest ye birds that round her sing,
  And welcome in the blooming year;
And doubly welcome be the Spring,
  The season to my Lucy dear.
    O wat ye wha's, etc.

The sun blinks blythe on yon town,   glances
  And on yon bonie braes of Ayr;
But my delight in yon town,
  And dearest bliss, is Lucy fair.
    O wat ye wha's, etc.

Without my love, not a' the charms
  O' Paradise could yield me joy;
But give me Lucy in my arms,
  And welcome Lapland's dreary sky.
    O wat ye wha's, etc.

My cave wad be a lover's bower,
    Tho' raging winter rent the air;
And she a lovely little flower,
    That I wad tent and shelter there.   *watch over*
        O wat ye wha's, etc.

O sweet is she in yon town,
    The sinkin' sun's gane down upon;
A fairer than's in yon town,
    His setting beam ne'er shone upon.
        O wat ye wha's, etc.

If angry fate is sworn my foe,
    And suffering I am doom'd to bear;
I careless quit aught else below;
    But, spare me—spare me, Lucy, dear!
        O wat ye wha's, etc.

For while life's dearest blood is warm,
    Ae thought frae her shall ne'er depart: *one . . . from*
And she—as fairest is her form,
    She has the truest, kindest heart.
        O wat ye wha's, etc.

Miss Lucy Johnston, in celebration of whose beauty and accomplishments the poet wrote this song, was the daughter of Wynne Johnston, Esq., of Hylton. It was originally dedicated to Jean Armour, but later by changing the name from Jean to Lucy he made it refer to Lucy Johnston. Having married Richard Alexander Oswald of Auchencruive in the county of Ayr, the poet first met her while residing with her husband in the neighbourhood of Dumfries, and in his character and out of compliment to him sought to do her honour.

It was well known that while under the influence of Jean Lorimer Burns composed many songs, and to suit a new lover he conveniently changed the name of the heroine. The above song is one of them.

Enclosing a copy of the song to Mr John Syme, Burns says:
'Do you know that among much that I admire in the characters and manners of those great folks whom I have now

the honour to call my acquaintances—the Oswald family, for instance—there is nothing charms me more than Mr Oswald's unconcealable attachment to that incomparable woman, his wife? In my song I have endeavoured to do justice to what would be his feelings on seeing, in the scene I have drawn, the habitation of his Lucy. As I am a good deal pleased with my performance, I, in my first fervour, thought of sending it to Mrs Oswald, but, on second thoughts, what I offer as the honest incense of genuine respect might, from the well-known character of poverty and poetry, be construed into some modification or other of that servility which my soul abhors.'

Mrs Oswald fell into ill health, and went to Lisbon to try to recuperate, but died there in January 1798, when she was only a little over thirty years of age.

The various encomiums which have been lavished on her are too numerous to be quoted. 'According to Dryden,' says Kirkpatrick Sharpe:

> Whate'er *she* did was done with so much ease,
> In *her* alone 'twas natural to please;
> Her motions all accompanied with grace;
> And Paradise was open'd in her face.

None who ever had the delight of seeing her in the ballroom, giving double charms to a minuet, or dignifying a country dance, can question the truth of this feeble encomium.' She was also an accomplished musician, and is said to have composed the air of Burns's song 'To Mary in Heaven' in which it is set.

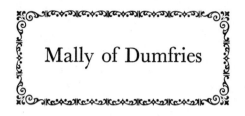

Mally of Dumfries

1795, age 36

O MALLY'S MEEK, MALLY'S SWEET

CHORUS

O Mally's meek, Mally's sweet,
Mally's modest and discreet,
Mally's rare, Mally's fair,
Mally's every way complete.

As I was walking up the street,
 A barefit maid I chanced to meet;   *barefoot*
But O the road was very hard
 For that fair maiden's tender feet.
 O Mally's meek, etc.

It were mair meet that those fine feet   *more*
 Were weel laced up in silken shoon;   *shoes*
And 'twere more fit that she should sit
 Within yon chariot gilt aboon.   *above*
 O Mally's meek, etc.

Her yellow hair, beyond compare,
 Comes trinkling down her swan-white neck; *trickling*
And her two eyes, like stars in skies,
 Wad keep a sinking ship frae wreck.   *would; from*
 O Mally's meek, etc.

BURNS was walking along the High Street, Dumfries, one day when he happened to meet a young lady from the country who was carrying her shoes and stockings, a custom in country districts not infrequent in the time of Burns, owing to their high cost, and to save them from wear and tear. She had her petti-coats kilted,

> Which did gently shaw
> Her straight bare legs that whiter were than snaw,

and was proceeding towards the Galloway side of the Nith. The Muse of the poet was so influenced by the unusual sight in a town like Dumfries, that there and then he composed the above short, exquisite lyric. 'Mally' is the Scottish form of 'Molly'.

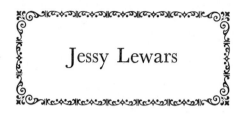

Jessy Lewars

1796, age 37

OH, WERT THOU IN THE CAULD BLAST

OH, wert thou in the cauld blast,	*cold*
On yonder lea, on yonder lea;	
My plaidie to the angry airt—	*direction*
I'd shelter thee, I'd shelter thee:	
Or did misfortune's bitter storms	
Around thee blaw, around thee blaw;	*blow*
Thy bield should be my bosom,	*shelter*
To share it a', to share it a'.	*all*

Or were I in the wildest waste,	
Sae bleak and bare, sae bleak and bare;	
The desert were a paradise,	
If thou wert there, if thou wert there:	
Or were I monarch o' the globe,	
Wi' thee to reign, wi' thee to reign;	
The brightest jewel in my crown	
Wad be my queen, wad be my queen.	*would*

THIS fine song is a tribute of the poet's Muse to his ministering angel—Miss Jessy Lewars. Her father died in 1789, when she was eleven years of age, and she had a brother, John, who later became Burns's fellow-exciseman at Dumfries. Jessy had quiet, motherly ways, and her amiable disposition greatly pleased the poet. She was also gifted as a singer. Referring to her in a letter to Mr James Johnson, June 1796, Burns says: 'My wife has a very particular friend of hers, a young lady who sings

well, to whom she wishes to present "The Scots Musical
Museum". If you have a spare copy, will you be so obliging as
to send it by the first "fly". R. B.'

In the early summer of 1796 Burns happened to pay a visit to
John Lewars, and suggested that if Jessy would play him a tune
she was fond of he would do his best to compose verses to it.
She accordingly sat down at the piano and played once or twice
the air of an old ditty beginning with the words:

> The robin cam' to the wren's nest,
>   And keekit in, and keekit in ;   *peeped*
> Oh, weel's me on your auld pow,   *well's; old head*
>   Wad ye be in, wad ye be in?   *would*
>
> Ye'se ne'er get leave to lie without, *you shall*
>   And I within, and I within,
> As lang's I hae an auld clout,   *as long as; old rag*
>   To row you in, to row you in.   *roll*

And after a few minutes' meditation he produced the song,
'Oh, Wert Thou in the Cauld Blast'. The song has been set to a
haunting tune by Mendelssohn, so that we have here a song by
a great poet and the music to it by a great musician.

Towards the end of his life the poet was unable to leave his
room, and as Jean Armour, his wife, was nearing her confine-
ment and consequently unable to attend to him, Jessy Lewars
took her place in the household. She greatly cheered and
comforted Burns, and he composed what Currie calls 'the last
offertory of his Muse in her honour':

HERE'S A HEALTH TO ANE I LO'E DEAR!

CHORUS

> *Here's a health to ane I lo'e dear!*
> *Here's a health to ane I lo'e dear!*
> *Thou art sweet as the smile when fond lovers meet,*
> *And soft as their parting tear—Jessy!*

Although thou maun never be mine,
  Although even hope is denied,
'Tis sweeter for thee despairing,
    Than aught in the world beside—Jessy!
      Here's a health, etc.

I mourn through the gay, gaudy day,
  As, hopeless, I muse on thy charms;
But welcome the dream o' sweet slumber,
    For then I am lockt in thy arms—Jessy!
      Here's a health, etc.

I guess by the dear angel smile,
  I guess by the love-rolling e'e;
But why urge the tender confession,
    'Gainst fortune's fell cruel decree—Jessy!
      Here's a health, etc.

Writing to Thomson, Burns says:

'This will be delivered by a Mr Lewars, a young fellow of uncommon merit: indeed by far the cleverest fellow I have met with in this part of the world. His only fault is d-m-cratic heresy. As he will be a day or two in town, you will have leisure, if you choose, to write me by him; and if you have a spare half-hour to spend with him, I shall place your kindness to my account. I have no copies of the songs I have sent you, and I have taken a fancy to review them all, and possibly may mend some of them; so, when you have complete leisure, I will thank you for either the originals or copies. I had rather be the author of five well-written songs than of ten otherwise. My verses to "Cauld Kail" I will suppress; as also those to "Laddie, lie near me". They are neither worthy of my name nor of your book. I have great hopes that the genial influence of the approaching summer will set me to rights, but as yet I cannot boast of returning health. I have now reason to believe that my complaint is a flying gout—a sad business!

'R.B.'

It is worthy of note here that this letter makes it quite clear that it was Burns's sincere wish to leave behind him a legacy of those songs only that were pure and good and elevating. Some songs he had hastily composed he greatly regretted, and asked that every song unworthy of his name and genius be consigned to irrevocable oblivion.

Three years after the poet's death Jessy married Mr James Thomson, a solicitor in Dumfries, and at a Festival in honour of the poet's sons held on 6th August 1844 on the banks of the Doon, Alloway, she and her husband were seated beside them in recognition of Jessy's loving ministry to their father.

After the death of her husband Jessy spent the remaining years of her life in Maxwelltown. She died on 26th May 1855, in her seventy-seventh year.

She is held in affectionate remembrance by all lovers of Burns. In the sunset of his life the poet himself thanked her for her loving service to him in his hour of bitter sorrow, anguish and suffering. His songs in her honour will keep her name and deeds long in the memory of mankind.

Her tombstone is fixed to the wall close to the Mausoleum of the National Bard in Dumfries.

JESSIE LEWARS
(*Page 143*)

OLD AYR

Miscellaneous Love Songs

1787, age 28

OF THE following popular song in praise of 'The Birks of Aberfeldy', Burns says: 'I composed these stanzas under the Falls of Moness, at or near Aberfeldy, 30th August 1787.' It is not known who 'the Bonie Lassie' was who 'supremely blest' the poet 'wi' her love'.

THE BIRKS OF ABERFELDY

CHORUS

Bonie lassie, will ye go
Will ye go, will ye go,
Bonie lassie, will ye go
 To the birks of Aberfeldy?   *birches*

Now Simmer blinks on flow'ry braes, *summer shines; slopes*
And o'er the crystal streamlets plays;
Come let us spend the lightsome days
In the birks of Aberfeldy.
 Bonie lassie, etc.

The little birdies blythely sing,
While o'er their heads the hazels hing, *hang*
Or lightly flit on wanton wing *flutter*
 In the birks of Aberfeldy.
 Bonie lassie, etc.

L

The braes ascend like lofty wa's,
The foamy stream deep-roaring fa's,
O'erhung wi' fragrant-spreading shaws,   *woods*
   The birks of Aberfeldy.
    Bonie lassie, etc.

The hoary cliffs are crown'd wi' flowers,
White o'er the linns the burnie pours,   *cascades*
And rising, weets wi' misty showers   *wets*
   The birks of Aberfeldy.
    Bonie lassie, etc.

Let Fortune's gifts at random flee,
They ne'er shall draw a wish frae me;   *from*
Supremely blest wi' love and thee
   In the birks of Aberfeldy.
    Bonie lassie, etc.

1792, age 33

MY WIFE'S A WINSOME WEE THING

CHORUS

She is a winsome wee thing,
She is a handsome wee thing,
She is a bonie wee thing.
   This sweet wee wife o' mine.

I NEVER saw a fairer,
I never lo'ed a dearer;
And neist my heart I'll wear her,   *next*
   For fear my jewel tine.   *be lost*
    She is, etc.

The warld's wrack we share o't.
The warstle and the care o't;   *struggle*
Wi' her I'll blythly bear it,
   And think my lot divine.
    She is, etc.

Yon Wild Mossy Mountains

Yon wild mossy mountains sae lofty and wide,
That nurse in their bosom the youth o' the Clyde,
Where the grouse lead their coveys through the heather to feed,
And the shepherd tends his flock as he pipes on his reed.
  Where the grouse lead their coveys through the heather to feed,
  And the shepherd tends his flock as he pipes on his reed.

Not Gowrie's rich valleys, nor Forth's sunny shores,
To me hae the charms o' yon wild mossy moors;
For there, by a lanely, sequester'd clear stream,
Resides a sweet lassie, my thought and my dream.
  For there, by a lanely, sequester'd clear stream,
  Resides a sweet lassie, my thought and my dream.

Amang thae wild mountains shall still be my path.   *those*
Ilk stream foaming down its ain green narrow strath;   *each*
For there, wi' my lassie, the day-lang I rove,
While o'er us, unheeded, flee the swift hours o' love.
  For there, wi' my lassie, the day-lang I rove,
  While o'er us, unheeded, flee the swift hours o' love.

She is not the fairest, although she is fair;
O' nice education but sma' is her share;
Her parentage humble as humble can be;
But I lo'e the dear lassie because she lo'es me.
  Her parentage humble as humble can be,
  But I lo'e the dear lassie, because she lo'es me.

To beauty what man but maun yield him a prize,   *must*
In her armour of glances, and blushes, and sighs?
And when wit and refinement hae polish'd her darts,
They dazzle our een as they flee to our hearts.   *eyes*
  And when wit and refinement hae polish'd her darts,
  They dazzle our een as they flee to our hearts.

But kindness, sweet kindness, in the fond sparkling ee,
Has lustre outshining the diamond to me;
And the heart-beating love, as I'm clasp'd in her arms,
Oh, these are my lassie's all-conquering charms?
    And the heart-beating love, as I'm clasp'd in her arms,
    Oh, these are my lassie's all-conquering charms!

Of this song Burns says: 'This song alludes to a part of my private history, which it is of no consequence to the world to know.' Stenhouse adds the remark that 'the reader on turning to the notes on the song entitled "The Highland Lassie, O" will have no difficulty in understanding that part of the bard's private history to which he alludes'. Allan Cunningham also ventures to agree with Stenhouse that 'Highland Mary' was the theme of the song.

We are inclined to agree, however, with Dr D. McNaught, in his *The Truth about Burns*, that all we know of the heroine of 'Yon Wild Mossy Mountains' is the allusion, in a letter to Gavin Hamilton, to 'a very pretty girl, a Lothian farmer's daughter', whom Burns had almost persuaded to accompany him to the West Country. City life was not congenial to his Muse, or it may have been that his recent feverish activity at Mossgiel had brought about a reaction.

1792, age 33

The Lea-rig

WHEN o'er the hill the eastern star,	
Tells bughtin-time is near, my jo,	*folding-time; my love*
And owsen frae the furrow'd field,	*oxen*
Return sae dowf and weary, O;	*slowly—dull*
Down by the burn, where scented birks	*birches*
Wi' dew are hanging clear, my jo,	
I'll meet thee on the lea-rig,	*strip of grass-land*
My ain kind dearie, O.	
In mirkest glen at midnight hour,	*darkest*
I'd rove, and ne'er be eerie, O,	*frightened*
If thro' that glen I gaed to thee,	*went*
My ain kind dearie, O:	

Altho' the night were ne'er sae wild,
   And I were ne'er sae weary, O,
I'd meet thee on the lea-rig,
   My ain kind dearie, O.

The hunter lo'es the morning sun,
   To rouse the mountain deer, my jo;
At noon the fisher seeks the glen,
   Along the burn to steer, my jo;
Gie me the hour o' gloamin' grey,   *twilight*
   It mak's my heart sae cheery, O,
To meet thee on the lea-rig,
   My ain kind dearie, O!   *own*

PRETTY PEG

As I gaed up by yon gate-end,   *went*
   When day was waxing weary,
Wha did I meet come down the street,
   But pretty Peg, my dearie?

Her air so sweet, her shape complete,
   Wi' nae proportion wanting,
The Queen of love could never move
   Wi' motion mair enchanting.

With linkèd hands we took the sands,
   Down by yon winding river;
And oh! that hour, and shady bow'r,
   Can I forget it?—Never!

1795, age 36

O LAY THY LOOF IN MINE, LASS

O LAY thy loof in mine, lass,   *palm of the hand*
In mine, lass, in mine, lass;
And swear on thy white hand, lass,
   That thou wilt be my ain.   *own*
A slave to love's unbounded sway,
He aft has wrought me meikle wae; *much; woe*
But now he is my deadly fae,   *foe*
   Unless thou be my ain.   *own*

There's mony a lass has broke my rest,
That for a blink I had lo'ed best;
But thou art queen within my breast,
    For ever to remain.
O lay thy loof in mine, lass,
    In mine, lass, in mine, lass;
And swear on thy white hand, lass,
    That thou wilt be my ain.

The Posie

(My ain dear May)

Burns in this song likens May to a posie of flowers: the primrose, the pink, the rose, the hyacinth, etc.

O, LUVE will venture in where it daur na weel be seen! *dare not well*
O, luve will venture in, where wisdom ance hath been!
But I will doun yon river rove amang the wood sae green.
    And a' to pu' a posie to my ain dear May!   *pull*

The primrose I will pu', the firstling o' the year,
And I will pu' the pink, the emblem o' my dear,
For she's the pink o' womankind, and blooms without a
    peer—
    And a' to be a posie to my ain dear May!

I'll pu' the budding rose when Phoebus peeps in view,
For it's like a baumy kiss o' her sweet, bonie mou.   *balmy*
The hyacinth's for constancy wi' its unchanging blue—
    And a' to be a posie to my ain dear May!

The lily it is pure, and the lily it is fair,
And in her lovely bosom I'll place the lily there.
The daisy's for simplicity and unaffected air—
    And a' to be a posie to my ain dear May!

The hawthorn I will pu', wi' its locks o' siller gray,   *silver*
Where, like an agèd man, it stands at break o' day;
But the songster's nest within the bush I winna tak' *will not*
    away—
    And a' to be a posie to my ain dear May!

The woodbine I will pu' when the e'ening star is near,
And the diamond draps o' dew shall be her een sae clear! *eyes so*
The violet's for modesty, which weel she fa's to wear— *claims*
    And a' to be a posie to my ain dear May!

I 'll tie the posie round wi' the silken band o' luve,
And I 'll place it in her breast, and I 'll swear by a' above,
That to my latest draught o' life the band shall ne'er
    remove,
    And this will be a posie to my ain dear May!

1794, age 35

CA' THE YOWES TO THE KNOWES

CHORUS

Ca' the yowes to the knowes,   call . . . ewes; hillocks, knolls
Ca' them whaur the heather grows,
Ca' them whaur the burnie rowes,   rolls
   My bonie dearie.

HARK, the mavis' evening sang   *song-thrush*
Sounding Clouden's woods amang!
Then a faulding let us gang,   *folding; go*
  My bonie dearie.
   Ca' the, etc.

We'll gae down by Clouden side,   *go; tributary of the Nith*
Thro' the hazels spreading wide,
O'er the waves, that sweetly glide
  To the moon sae clearly.
   Ca' the, etc.

Yonder Clouden's silent towers,   *ruined abbey of Linclouden*
Where at moonshine midnight hours,
O'er the dewy bending flowers,
  Fairies dance sae cheerie.
   Ca' the, etc.

Ghaist nor bogle shalt thou fear;   *ghost nor hobgoblin*
Thou'rt to love and heaven sae dear,
Nocht of ill may come thee near,   *nothing*
  My bonie dearie.
    Ca' the, etc.

Fair and lovely as thou art,
Thou hast stown my very heart;   *stolen*
I can die—but canna part,
  My bonie dearie.
    Ca' the, etc.

SWEETEST MAY

SWEETEST May, let love inspire thee;
Take a heart which he desires thee;
As thy constant slave regard it;
For its faith and truth reward it.

Proof o' shot to birth or money,
Not the wealthy, but the bonie;
Not high-born, but noble-minded,
In love's silken band can bind it!

1793, age 34

A RED, RED ROSE

This sweet song was composed by Burns, and is connected with words by Lieut. Hinches as a farewell to his sweetheart on the eve of parting. It first appeared in Johnson's *Museum*, 1796, with Burns's name attached, and is sung to one of the sweetest of Scottish airs, 'Low down he's in the broom'. Without trying it, the poet reproduced the ancient style in a manner better than even the most skilled manufacturer of reliques could hope to approach. The verses were introduced by Terry into his musical drama of *Rob Roy*, and when that play was first produced in London the song was, for the time, the reigning favourite in the metropolis.

O MY luve's like a red, red rose
    That's newly sprung in June;
O my luve's like the melodie
    That's sweetly play'd in tune.

As fair art thou, my bonie lass,
    So deep in luve am I;
And I will luve thee still, my dear,
    Till a' the seas gang dry.   *go*

Till a' the seas gang dry, my dear,
    And the rocks melt wi' the sun:
O I will love thee still, my dear,
    While the sands o' life shall run.

And fare-thee-weel, my only luve!
    And fare-thee-weel awhile!
And I will come again, my luve,
    Tho' 'twere ten thousand mile!

O my luve's like a red, red rose
    That's newly sprung in June;
O my luve's like the melodie
    That's sweetly play'd in tune.

In conclusion we agree with Whittier that Robert Burns lives on with a vitality which gathers strength from time. His fame broadens and deepens every year. The world has never known a truer singer.